Tales from Nebraska Sidelines

A Collection of the Greatest Nebraska Stories Ever Told

By

Don (Fox) Bryant

Sports Publishing, L.L.C.
www.SportsPublishingllc.com

Director of production: Susan M. Moyer
Senior project manager, book design: Jennifer L. Polson
Dust jacket design: Kenneth O'Brien

ISBN: 1-58261-326-5

Printed in the United States.

SPORTS PUBLISHING, L.L.C.
www.SportsPublishingLLC.com

Dedication

*One does not spend 50 years in sportswriting
and college athletics administration without working
long hours, nights and weekends.
Family time is at the mercy of the "Impossible Mission,"
and it is a blessing to have an understanding,
loving and supportive family.*

*Such a blessing has been provided me by my wonderful wife of
50 years, Pedie (whose real name is Joan),
sons Bill and Jeff, their wives Linda and Jean,
and four beloved grandchildren—Jason, Jennifer, Jessica and Asa.*

*To them this book is dedicated
with all the love and gratitude Old Fox can muster.*

—"Fox," Dad and Grandpa

Acknowledgments

Lincoln, Nebraska
March 15, 2001

No one who ever worked in sports information or any other area of intercollegiate athletics could enjoy any measure of success without the help of others. I am forever in debt to secretaries, student-assistants, full-time assistants and, of course, coaches, athletes, university administrators and Regents.

But I must give special thanks to Janette Sojka, my secretary and co-worker for 20 years; Vicki Cartwright, the sports information office manager for that time and more; Tom "Mini Fox" Simons, my first full-time assistant and long-time friend.

Thanks also to Tippy Dye, who hired me; Bob Devaney, Tom Osborne and Tom Solich, all of whom made working with Nebraska football teams a joy; present athletic direction Bill Bryne; and all the countless co-workers, media friends and fans who made life in the caldron of Cornhusker life a wonderful experience.

—"Fox"

Contents

Acknowledgments *4*

Foreword *6*

Introduction *7*

Chapter 1
The Early Days:
From Bugeaters to Cornhuskers 9

Chapter 2
Devaney Enters, Success Follows 31

Chapter 3
Osborne 51

Chapter 4
Husker Heroes 71

Chapter 5
Going Bowling 109

Chapter 6
Planes, Trains & Automobiles 127

Chapter 7
Strike Up the Band 137

Chapter 8
Husker Potpourri 149

Chapter 9
Memories from the Press Box 157

Chapter 10
Fox Tales 171

Foreword

If you want any kind of story about Cornhuskers football across the last half century, there is only one ultimate source.

That would be Don Bryant, alias the (now) Silver Fox. If he doesn't know what you looking for, it probably doesn't exist.

At worst he certainly knows where to find it and quickly.

The Fox, in my opinion, is the mold for the successful Sports Information Director. I've been broadcasting college football games since 1952 from every nook and cranny of the country, just in case you feel that opinion needed a little muscle.

College football, as much as any other activity, is part of the fabric of our society, and especially the legendary domain of Big Red football.

Fox didn't coach 'em on the field, but he certainly helped shape the presentation and sell the product.

I'm sure you will enjoy his reflections and recollections.

—Keith Jackson

Introduction

Some 40 years ago, a former Nebraska Cornhusker quarterback in the late 1930s offered me some advice that I've meant to take for quite some time. Thurston Phelps, old No. 27 and a boyhood hero of mine, saw me at a banquet and said:

"You're a fine sports editor and you are writing every day about history—just don't wait too long to write your book!"

Good friend "Thursty" has been gone for many years, but I've never forgotten his admonition. Since retirement as associate athletics director at the University of Nebraska in the summer of 1997, many Husker fans and friends have asked on numerous occasions, "When are you going to write a book? You've got all those stories about the Cornhuskers, the Olympics, the Final Fours, pro baseball, Coach Bob Devaney, Coach Tom Osborne—I'd love to read those stories."

So, at long last, I've tried to tell the stories that have helped to make life exciting, interesting and fun for me during my 50-plus years as a sports writer, sports editor, sports information director and university athletic administrator. The stories are about people and behind the scenes activities—not about wins and losses.

In 1971, my good friend Johnny Keith (then Oklahoma's hustling SID) and I learned that the way to cope with the intense pressures associated with the great OU–Nebraska football rivalry was simple: We never let a game ruin a good week.

Actually, I think that philosophy has enabled me—and a great many others in athletics—to survive and continually enjoy going to work in the wacky world of American sports year after year. Survivors don't live or die with each athletic contest.

Hopefully, readers will enjoy anecdotes about my friends and our half-century adventures—and also come to the realization that there is a great deal more to athletics at all levels than final scores.

—Don Bryant
Associate AD/SID Emeritus
University Of Nebraska

1

The Early Days:
From Bugeaters to Cornhuskers

All-Time All-American Weir

In his roundup of the 1940 season, sports editor "Cy" Sherman paid tribute to Ed Weir, writing, "Weir, as a matter of course, merits particular recognition here, inasmuch as he rates in the writer's private book as Nebraska's all-time All-American." The late Knute Rockne apparently accorded Weir similar appraisal, as it was

Ed Weir

due to Rockne's judgment that the present head coach of track at Nebraska was listed in 1924 and 1925 as a first-team tackle by the 'All-America Football Board.'"

Ed Weir remains one of the most revered Cornhuskers of all time. Many more would follow his lead in the decades to come.

Early Coaches

Nebraska's football stature continued to grow in the 1930s under Dana X. Bible, who arrived in Lincoln in 1929, won six Big Six Conference titles, and departed for Texas after the 1936 season. D.X. achieved Hall of Fame status at Nebraska and nationally, but he didn't beat Pittsburgh or Minnesota during his Cornhusker reign.

Lawrence McCeney "Biff" Jones took care of those matters before departing for World War II duty as an Army major in 1942. Jones coached the Army Cadets to victory over Nebraska in 1928, knocking the Cornhuskers out of a Rose Bowl bid, but Nebraska fans forgave The Major after his first game in 1937 when the Huskers beat Bernie Bierman's Minnesota Gophers, 14-9.

Biff Jones would take a team to the Rose Bowl—Nebraska, after the 1940 season, but it took a building program, patience, and hard work.

1941 Rose Bowl

Nebraskans have long cherished the memory of the 1940 Cornhuskers, who lost only to national champion Minnesota and gained a Rose Bowl bid to meet Stanford on January 1, 1941. It was a football moment to treasure, particularly the pride that came from the fact that every player on the squad, with the exception of fullback Vike Francis, came through the high school ranks in Nebraska. Francis, like his brother Sam, who was an All-America fullback and Olympic shot-putter in 1936, hailed from the Nebraska-Kansas border town of Oberlin.

It was a homegrown bunch of Cornhuskers who went west to battle Clark Shaughnessey's Stanford Indians, and so what if they got beat 21-13? "Our kids gave 'em a real battle," was a familiar statement in Nebraska coffee shops for many years.

Never Say Never

Forrest Behm, a Lincoln native, epitomized the Nebraska players of that "Rose Bowl Era." Mainly because he had all the attributes of an All-American boy, which he became, even though he almost never had an opportunity to play football. Forry did both play and make All-America by overcoming impossible odds.

Badly burned in a backyard bonfire when he was five years old, doctors wanted to amputate his damaged left leg. But his father refused to let the amputation take place. Rather, Mr. Behm would send his family out of the house, then wrap his hands in cotton and massage his son's leg night after night. It would be years before Forry could walk without crutches, braces, and canes. Athletics seemed out of the question, but finally after years of agony, Forry Behm was able to play some football in his senior year at Lincoln High School.

Forrest Behm

He enrolled at the University of Nebraska and went out for the freshman team. However, equipment manager Floyd Bottorff did not have any size 13 shoes, so Mr. Behm special ordered a pair of football shoes for his son, and a Cornhusker legend was born. Coach Biff Jones started a rebuilding program in 1938, basing the future on a group of talented sophomores that included Forry Behm. Forry started every game at tackle for three seasons, as Nebraska marched to the Rose Bowl. During his senior season, he earned All-Big Six and All-America honors, as well as being named Honorary Commandant of the ROTC and Homecoming King. After service with the U.S. Army in World War, the Nebraska boy who couldn't play football but did, started on the production line at Corning Glass Company and rose to become president of Corning International.

Thanks to a father who wouldn't let his leg be amputated, years of rehabilitation, and a burning love for the game of football, Forrest Behm was elected to the National Football Foundation's College Football Hall of Fame in 1980.

From the Rose Bowl to the Future

Rose Bowl team seniors who joined Behm against Stanford included All-America guard Warren Alfson, All-Big Six stars End Ray Prochaska, Halfbacks Walter "Butch" Luther, and Harry "Hippity" Hopp, quarterback Roy Petsch, and fullback Vike Francis.

Other seniors included Halfback Herman Rohrig, quarterback George "Bus" Knight, halfback Theos Thompson, center Bob Burress, guard Leonard Muskin and the Kahler tackle brothers, Royal and Robert.

These 1938 sophomores made sure Biff Jones' three-year dream plan became a reality in 1940. Like Behm, they all made their marks in life. Prochaska had a long coaching career at Nebraska and the NFL, while Hermie Rohrig became an NFL official before serving for years at supervisor of officials for the Big 10 Conference. Warren Alfson became a successful Nebraska cattle feeder, and "Bus" Knight a bank president.

"Butch" Luther, whose 57-yard touchdown run against Iowa State opened the door for the coveted Rose Bowl invitation, did not survive the war. An Army captain, he was killed in action during the Italian campaign following the Anzio invasion. All-Conference guard Eddie Schwartzkopf was a junior and returned from WWII duty to letter again in 1946. Later he served for many years as a distinguished University of Nebraska Regent.

Go Bugeaters!?

Nebraska football did not start with D.X. Bible or Biff Jones, nor Bob Devaney or Tom Osborne. There were the early days when college football was in its infancy, the 1890s, and Nebraska was there, but was not known as the Cornhuskers. That would not become reality until 1899, when Charles "Cy" Sherman adopted the name dropped by the University of Iowa. Cy was a sportswriter for the *Nebraska State Journal* at the time, but he gained his real fame as the pugnacious sports editor of *The Lincoln Star.*

During the years until his retirement in 1947, Cy battled for fair play, honesty, and his beloved Nebraska Cornhuskers with his pen in his column, "Brass Tacks." Sherman could be like a bulldog chewing on a pant leg when he launched a crusade, and one he played a key role in was bedeviling the *Associated Press* into starting a college football poll. The AP capitulated to Sherman and his fellow sports editors who wanted a poll in 1936.

Prior to Sherman's baptism of "Cornhuskers," the Nebraska football team had known by various nicknames like "Rattlesnake Boys," "Old Gold Knights," "Antelopes" and "Bugeaters" (for Prairie Bats). Whatever they were called, Nebraska teams started making history as the 20th century drew near.

Segregated Cornhuskers

One of the earliest African-American athletes to play college football was Nebraska's George Flippin, who starred from 1891 to 1894. Flippin later would become a medical doctor and surgeon in Stromsburg, Nebraska. He led NU to a 6-0 win over Illinois to open the 1892 season, but a scheduled game with the University of Missouri at Omaha in November was canceled. Mis-

George Flippin

souri players refused to meet a team that had a Black player, and the game still stands in the record book as a 1-0 forfeit to Nebraska.

Nebraska would not have a similar racial problem until the 1950s, when African-Americans were becoming welcome on college campuses. But not everywhere.

The Cornhuskers had three Black players in 1954—Charles Bryant, Jon McWilliams, and Sylvester Harris—and when the team went to Oklahoma to meet the Sooners, the trio was banned from staying in the team hotel.

After a prolonged argument with the manager in the lobby, athletic director Bill Orwig and Coach Bill Glassford did achieve a compromise that to this day points to the segregation ills of the era. The Black players could eat meals with the team but had to sleep at the Black YMCA. Trainer Paul Schneider escorted the trio to the YMCA, and at mealtime they were driven by cab to the hotel alley, walked through the kitchen, ate with their teammates, returned to the alley via the kitchen and rode in a cab with trainer Schneider back to the YMCA to sleep.

Left to right: Sylvester Harris, Charles Bryant, Ralph Fox, Paul Schneider, John McWilliams, and George Sullivan (Photo courtesy of Lincoln Journal and Star).

All three became solid citizens, achieving success in teaching, coaching, and business, despite the humiliation they endured to gain an education and play college football. Happily, Charley Bryant, an All-Big Seven guard, and Jon McWilliams, an All-Conference end, now reside in the Nebraska Football Hall of Fame.

Pound for Football

Roscoe Pound, who would one day become Dean of Harvard Law, had a passion for football during his tenure on the University of Nebraska faculty.

Speculation continues that Dean Pound, who wanted no part of the growing feminist movement in the United States, pushed football as a means to combat his sister, Louise. Also a member of the faculty, Louise was a leader in the feminist war and a staunch opponent of the brutal sport of football, according to tales from the 19th century.

Handwritten minutes of the Athletic Board meetings in the 1890s are filled with actions proposed by Dean Pound and adopted by the board. At one meeting it was noted that Dean Pound had been successful in persuading star running back Maurice Benedict to return to the team after learning that Benedict had indicated a desire to drop football and concentrate on his academic studies.

Among Pound's other football causes: Gaining approval of a motion to appoint a committee to stage a benefit show to "provide for the football team" and another committee appointed to "press the Regents to resist encroachments upon the athletic fields in the coming year of 1896."

As a sign of things to come years later, Dean Pound put the Athletic Board's feet to the fire by motioning and gaining approval of the lofty sum of "$10 a week for a football training table." Big-time days definitely were approaching for Nebraska football.

Fielding Yost

Nebraska's 1898 Bugeaters posted a sparkling 8-3-0 record, and the Athletic Board had no problem in loosening up the purse strings. They approved without dissent Fielding H. Yost's bill for $340 he submitted for coaching Nebraska to a record eight-win season. But 1898 was Yost's only season at Nebraska. He departed for the University of Michigan, where he would achieve "Point-A-Minute" fame and a long tenure as one of the nation's most respected coaches. Yost was inducted into the National Football Foundation's College Football Hall of Fame in 1951, representing both the University of Nebraska and the University of Michigan.

Money Matters

In 1899 there was no athletic director at the University of Nebraska, but the football team finances were handled by the "team manager." Board minutes reveal that in November, Mr. Collett reported the football team was having "a very successful season financially and anticipated from $50 to $75 profit for the season." A month later, the team manager reported the football team would be "about $25 ahead for the season." A century later, the Nebraska athletic department's budget was in the $40-million bracket.

"Bummy" Booth

With the arrival of a new century in 1900, Nebraska football took a huge step toward prominence in the world of college football. Prior to the start of the season, the NU Athletic Board called a special meeting to hire a new coach to succeed Fielding Yost. Candidates, according to the minutes, were Edgar E. Clinton, Walter C. Booth, Earnest C. White, and W.C. Milford. Incidentally, Milford had been the captain of the 1898 team and wound up being censured by the Board for playing an ineligible man in a game with the Denver Athletic Club in Denver. Actually, the Board had forbidden the team to make the trip to Denver in the first place, because the Denver AC was not a college team.

Milford's chances of getting the coaching job apparently were slim or none after that, because Walter Booth from Princeton University was the unanimous choice of the Board. That action prompted Dr. Lees to move that the Board "offer Mr. Booth $500 dollars and railroad fare one way." That, of course, was a jump of $160 over Yost, but the daring salary hike turned out to be a very worthwhile investment by the NU Athletic Board.

The new Cornhusker coach became famous as "Bummy" Booth, and he still ranks as the second-winningest coach in Nebraska history. During a six-year stay, his NU teams won 46, lost only eight, and tied one and produced a 24-game winning streak between 1901 and 1904. That still stands as a Husker record. Bob Devaney's teams won 22 straight during a 32-game unbeaten streak between 1969 and the 1972 opener at UCLA. Booth's .845 winning percentage trails only E.O. "Jumbo" Stiehm's .913 (1911-1915) and is just ahead of Tom Osborne's .836 (1973-1997).

Rising Prices

With the expenses of football at Nebraska rising as coaching salaries escalated in 1900, the Athletic Board was forced to take drastic action. Ticket prices for the Thanksgiving Day game with Minnesota were raised to 75 cents for general admission and $1 for reserved seats in the grandstand. Parking for Husker football fans was a problem in 1900, just as it remains today. The

Athletic Board also established a 50-cent charge for vehicles fans used to watch the game in comfort—automobiles or buggies? There was good news for the players, if not for the fans. The Board authorized an increase in football letter sweaters from 13 to 15, a trend that continues to this day.

Charlie Brock, 1936-38

Wally Provost, longtime sports editor and columnist for the *Omaha World Herald,* was one of the finest wordsmiths in the newspaper business until his death. He loved college football, and in 1971 he helped found the Nebraska Chapter of the National Football Foundation, as well as the Nebraska Football Hall of Fame, which started in 1971.

Long a fan of Charley Brock, Nebraska center in 1936-37-38, Wally provided a column for the *Hickman Voice,* which paid high tribute to the 1937 All-American.

"Charley was without question one of the greatest linebackers in NU history," Wally wrote. "Press box graybeards . . . whose firsthand knowledge of the Huskers went all the way back to the turn of the century, said Brock made more pass interceptions than any other center in NU annals . . . Brock stepped into a starting job with Green Bay and helped the club win the pro championship . . . He intercepted two passes in the title game . . ."

Who would have guessed in 1900 that (1) University of Nebraska athletic teams would be known worldwide as "Cornhuskers" and (2) the Huskers would take 177 players and an airplane load of staff and family members to play Northwestern University in the Alamo Bowl? And that the team would start the 2001 season with 58 lettermen on the roster? Even Roscoe Pound could not have forseen such growth in his cherished football program.

What Would the Fans Say?

Nebraska's 1940 team, forever known as the "Rose Bowl Team," held a 60th anniversary reunion during the 2000 Homecoming weekend of the Husker-Kansas game.

A gallant band of old warriors gathered at the Alumni Association's Wick Center for a banquet that produced tall tales aplenty.

Hall of Fame tackle Forrest Behm reminded everyone of his role in making sure the Cornhuskers accepted the Rose Bowl bid.

"I was a student member of the Athletic Board, and there was hesitation on the part of the faculty, which was concerned about lost class time," Forry recalled. "I interjected and asked, what will you tell all the fans in the towns across Nebraska if you refuse to let the team go to the Rose Bowl?"

Grinning, he added, "The room got real quiet—and we went to Pasadena!"

The Lone Aerial TD

Herman Rohrig, who became a college and NFL football official before serving as supervisor of Big 10 officials for years, referred to the record book and announced, "I am still the only Nebraska player to throw a touchdown pass in the Rose Bowl!"

Not to be undone, Al Zikmund, who retired after long service at Kearney State (now University of Nebraska-Kearney) as football coach and later athletic director, noted, "I am the only Nebraska player to catch a touchdown pass in the Rose Bowl!"

Rohrig's pass to Zikmund for a 33-yard TD broke a 7-7 tie with Stanford in the second quarter, but the PAT kick was blocked, and the Indians went ahead to take a 14-13 lead at halftime. Pete Kmetovic's 39-yard punt return for a touchdown after Nebraska's famed goal-line stand in the fourth quarter gave Stanford a 21-13 victory.

Rohrig and Zikmund, who broke his leg in the game, can also boast that they are the only players in conference history to hook up for an aerial touchdown in the Rose Bowl. Nebraska is the only team in conference history to play in the Rose Bowl game, and the 92,000 fans who saw the Husker-Stanford battle still rank as the largest crowd in Nebraska history.

Cousin Paul

Nebraska fans are renowned for 1) good sportsmanship most of time; 2) friendly relations with opposing fans home and away, and 3) being knowledgeable about the game of football.

Husker fans who sit in the northwest corner of Memorial Stadium above the field entrance used by visiting teams, traditionally stand and applaud the visiting players and coaches—win or lose—as they leave the field after games.

In 1977, Paul "Bear" Bryant brought his Alabama team to Lincoln to play Tom Osborne's Huskers. It was his first visit to Memorial Stadium since 1955, when his Texas A&M team beat Nebraska, 27-0. That was my first meeting with the legendary coach, and it occurred during a traumatic season that would end with Bill Glassford resigning as Nebraska's head coach.

Nebraska had lost to Hawaii, 6-0 in the opener, largely because Glassford had beaten the Rainbows 50-0 in 1954 and would face Ohio State the next week. The Huskers spent fall camp prepping for the Buckeyes and scared Ohio State before falling, 28-20. Nebraska then beat Kansas State before facing the Aggies. I met the A&M plane at the airport and asked to interview Coach Bryant for *The Lincoln Star,* but he asked me to come to his hotel.

Coach Bryant gave me a fine interview, and after his team beat Nebraska, I went to his locker room at the southeast corner of Memorial Stadium.

He spotted me and said, "Cousin Don, come here. I've got only one thing to say, Coach Glassford deserves to be coach of the year for getting that bunch of kids to play Ohio State as well as they did." He indicated Nebraska didn't have much talent but had a lot of nice young men.

My story quoting "Cousin Paul" resulted in the Husker players hanging me in effigy in Schulte Field House the next week. Dick Becker of *The Lincoln Journal* and I became branded as the "Bobsey Twins" by the Huskers, and relations between Glassford, most of his assistants and the players, and the media remained strained throughout the season. The Huskers wound up a solid 5-5 after the Hawaii stunner, a tribute to Coach Glassford and his players who pulled together when things were darkest.

George Flippin

Husker football fans frequently supply little-known anecdotes. Max Peterson of Dayton, Ohio, delivered a historical note about George Flippin after reading about the first African-American Nebraska football player.

Flippin lettered at Nebraska in 1892-93-94 and later became a physician in Stromsburg, Nebraska. In his first season on the football team, George gained a place in history when the University of Missouri team refused to play the scheduled game with Nebraska in Omaha because of Flippin's presence. The game is still listed as 1-0 forfeit to Nebraska.

Flippin Team Photo

An ex-Nebraska track letterman, Peterson wrote, "I wanted to tell you my dad knew Flippin. He gave my dad a shot in "You Know Where" when dad was a kid in Stromsburg."

Undefeated Frothy

When a college football program has been so successful as Nebraska's since the arrival of Bob Devaney in 1962, it's no surprise when fans start expecting undefeated seasons and conference and national No. 1 rankings every year.

However, that expectation is very difficult for a coach to deliver. Tough even once, twice, or three times in 25 years, but definitely a long shot every year.

Only one Nebraska coach since 1890 has produced an unbeaten team in his first season—Dr. Langdon Frothingham in 1890, NU's first season. Old Frothy set the mark with a 2-0 record, beating the Omaha YMCA (10-0) and Crete's Doane College (18-0). Note that any future coach must not only go undefeated in his rookie season, but also go unscored upon in order to erase Frothingham in the record book.

Winning all the games in a season takes outstanding players, smart coaching, good scheduling, acceptable weather, and some good luck, to boot.

Only four other Husker coaches have managed to post unbeaten seasons, and Tom Osborne is the undisputed leader. Dr. Tom—now Congressman Tom—piled up three in four years (1994-1995 and 1997). Walter "Bummy" Booth matched Osborne in back-to-back undefeated seasons (1902 and 1903), while Ewald O. "Jumbo" Stiehm was unbeaten in 1913 and 1915. Bob Devaney's 1970 and 1971 teams were undefeated, but the 1970 team had a 21-21 tie with Southern California. Both NU teams, however, won No. 1 rankings.

Slippery Pads

Nebraska's first football game on television was the 1953 season opener with the Oregon Ducks. It may still rank as the longest college television game without an overtime.

Mel Allen was on hand at Memorial Stadium to provide the play-by-play, and years later in the press lounge at Yankee Stadium, Mel recalled the game and said, "That's one of the longest games I've ever done."

Longtime Husker trainer and physical therapist George Finley Sullivan tells about the problems encountered on that hot September afternoon at Memorial Stadium:

"We had those shiny gold pants, and the pockets were not right. Coach Bill Glass felt it would make our kids run better if we taped the pads on their legs instead of stuffing the pads in the pants.

"Our equipment manager, Floyd Bottorff, had covered the thigh pads with some new naugahide, and that made them slick. We taped the pads on the players' legs, but they would sweat, and the tape would slip off the pads.

"We almost broke Bob Smith's leg that day," Sullivan said.

"He was running, and the pads slipped down over his knees."

What made the game so long was the fact Nebraska had to have an equipment time-out every few plays because of slipped pads. Players would make a circle around a player with slipped pads who would drop his pants. Trainers Sullivan and Paul Schneider would re-tape the pads on the player's leg.

"We finally got the game over," Sullivan said. "But Oregon won the game (20-12), and we didn't make a real hit with the TV folks."

Smith, a Grand Island native, earned All-Big 7 fullback honors in 1954. He was inducted into the Nebraska Football Hall of Fame in 1996.

2

Devaney Enters,
Success Follows

Devaney Comes to Nebraska

Robert S. Devaney ("rhymes with fanny," as Bob often reminded folks) rescued Nebraska's football program from the depths of a depression that lasted from 1940 until his arrival from Wyoming in 1962.

A jovial and impish Irishman who left a Michigan high school career to apprentice with Duffy Daugherty at Michigan State before winning big at Wyoming, Devaney launched a football revival that would be the envy of Billy Graham's staff.

Nebraskans yearned for football respect of the kind generated by their beloved Rose Bowl team of 1940, but only three winning seasons (1950, 1952, and 1954) and a .500 mark in 1955 were in the record book when Devaney succeeded Bill Jennings after the 1961 season.

Devaney stunned the nation by going 9-2 with a Gotham Bowl win over George Mira and Miami in his debut, then won four straight Big Eight titles.

After a pair of 6-4 years, he won four more league crowns and two national championships before retiring and picking Tom Osborne as his successor.

Devaney, whose record at Wyoming (35-10-5) and Nebraska (101-20-2) combined shows 12 conference titles, two national championships, and a 7-3 bowl record, earned his induction into the College Football Hall of Fame in 1981. Bob might have had a successful political career, considering his comical talent on the stump and a sensational football resume, but he chose to build a remarkable overall athletic program as athletic director. He succeeded Tippy Dye in 1967 and held the AD reins until 1993 when he became athletic director emeritus until his death in 1997.

Dr. Tom

Tom Osborne became the heir apparent to Devaney's head coach chair after the 1972 Orange Bowl game, which saw the Huskers bulldoze Bear Bryant's Alabama team, 38-6. That clinched a second-straight national No. 1 ranking after a brilliant season that featured Nebraska's 35-31 win over No. 2 Oklahoma in the still-remembered "Game of the Century."

After disposing of No. 2 Alabama, Devaney announced that the 1972 season would be his last. He named Osborne assistant head coach and, exercising his AD powers (no doubt with the approval of Chancellor D.B. "Woody" Varner and the Board of Regents) informed the world that Dr. (Ph.D.) Tom would be the next Cornhusker head coach.

Devaney lived to see Osborne measure up to his expectations: a 25-year career that resulted in 255 wins, 49 losses and three ties; 25 years in the national rankings, 25 bowl appearances, 12 conference championships and three national titles.

Game of the Century

My most memorable football game is the 1971 Nebraska-Oklahoma "Game of the Century" battle at Norman. Nebraska rallied in the final eight minutes with a long drive after Jack Mildren put OU ahead 31-28 with a touchdown pass. Husker quarterback Jerry Tagge handed off to Jeff Kinney on every play but one, a desperation third-down pass to Johnny Rodgers, who made a diving catch to keep the drive alive. Kinney plunged over from the three for a winning margin, 35-31, and the Black Shirt defense—led by All-America tackle Larry Jacobson and All-America middle guard Rich Glover—swamped the Sooners in the final seconds to clinch a solid No. 1 ranking heading to Hawaii for the final regular-season game and the Orange Bowl game with Alabama.

Oklahoma SID Johnny Keith and I were fortunate to survive the week, let alone the magnificent struggle between the No. 1 Huskers and the No. 2 Sooners. By Monday prior to the game, some 100 media representatives were in Norman, eager for copy and interviews and nighttime R and R. We arranged press conferences and interviews on both campuses, as well as lunches, dinners, and bistro revelry in Oklahoma City and Norman, resulting in a week of 20-hour days.

Exhausted but resilient, we made it to the game, but barely. After the Sooners went ahead once again in the fourth quarter, I was standing on the sidelines during Nebraska's historic victory drive. Cold and weary and with tension building on every Jeff Kinney plunge, I kept telling myself, "Don't have a heart attack. . . . Don't have a stroke. . . . Be professional and a good sport when we lose the game. . . . Don't have a heart attack." As the Huskers drew nearer the Sooner end zone, Campbell-Ewald executive John Bluth, who handled ABC sponsor Chevrolet's advertising, rushed up to me and asked, "Fox, how can you be calm at a time like this?"

The "Game of the Century" was Bob Devaney's signature coaching triumph. His Huskers had won a national title in 1970 by beating LSU, 17-12, in the Orange Bowl after the top two teams in the nation lost New Year's Day bowl games. Nebraska opened the 1971 season ranked No. 2, beat Oregon, 34-7, in the opener and vaulted to No. 1 and stayed there for a 13-0 record.

But the victory at Oklahoma was the supreme test, and after surviving in Norman against a great OU team ranked No. 2, the Huskers were prepared to dismantle Bear Bryant's Alabama team, 38-6, in the Orange Bowl.

In the days before conference alignments and the BCS, bowl lineups were up for grabs. Bowl committees competed for the top teams, and schools campaigned for the top bowl bids. Heading into the 1971 OU-Nebraska game, with Nebraska No. 1 and Oklahoma No. 2, the winner by virtue of the Big Eight Conference contract with the Orange Bowl was guaranteed a trip to Miami. But what about the loser? The Sugar Bowl, then led by executive director Joe Katz, a retired U.S. Navy captain, was actively courting both teams to ensure landing one of the top two teams in the nation.

Bob Devaney, also Nebraska's athletic director, had a strong desire to return to Miami and applied pressure on Oklahoma to make a deal. As a result, the two schools settled bowl plans before the Thanksgiving Day battle. Whatever the outcome, Nebraska would get the Orange Bowl bid, and Oklahoma was set for the Sugar Bowl.

Criticized in some quarters for accepting Oklahoma early instead of waiting for the outcome of the game, the Sugar Bowl took the position that it had hooked up with the best team and would have a top bowl game with Oklahoma.

Joe Katz was quoted extensively with the boast, "Oklahoma will beat Nebraska by 20 points."

Poor Joe, a good friend and fun guy to work with in bowl dealings, had that quote come back to haunt him after the "Game of the Century," which Nebraska won, 35-31.

Bob and I fought our way through the milling crowd to the media interview room, where Sugar Bowl director Joe Katz stood by the door. As Devaney moved into the room, Joe extended his hand and said, "Congratulations, Bob."

Without breaking stride, Devaney replied, "Stick those 20 points up your ass!"

The Red Rabbit's Foot

Superstition plays a big part in college football. Tom Osborne is the only coach I can remember disavowing the use of superstitious methods to win football games. Tom believed firmly that you win football games by working hard, preparing for every possible situation, playing hard and being better conditioned than an opponent, especially in the fourth quarter.

All those things really worked well for Tom, and it didn't bother me that he felt that silly superstitions should not be part of his game plan. He became Nebraska's all-time winningest coach (255 victories in 25 years), but Bob Devaney and I always tried to get Tom a little extra help.

In December of 1968, I was the adult advisor to the Golden Sun Order of the Arrow Lodge (Cornhusker Council, Boy Scouts of America.) At a meeting of the Lodge, the boys presented me with a red rabbit's foot for good luck. It stayed unlucky in a drawer until the fifth game of the 1969 season. The Kansas Jayhawks came to Lincoln after the Huskers had lost to USC, beaten Texas A&M and Minnesota, and lost to Missouri in the first Big Eight game of the year. Nebraska had gone 6-4 in 1967 and 1968, and considerable heat from fans and the NU Regents was on Bob to prove the game had not passed him by.

Prior to the game in the coaches' dressing room, I happened to pull my keys out of a pocket, and the red rabbit's foot fell on the floor. I still don't know why I had it that day, but Devaney spotted it and asked, "What the hell is that?" I told him, and he said, "Let me rub it, we need all the luck we can get." The coaches and I laughed, and everyone went to work.

Late in the game, with KU leading, 17-14, Jerry Tagge heaved a desperation pass, and Kansas was called for interference, which resulted in a Jayhawk player calling the official a naughty word, and the Huskers were so close to the goal they couldn't help but win, 21-17. A week later, Bob asked me for the rabbit's foot again before the game, and NU beat Oklahoma State, 13-3.

Coach Robert rubbed the red rabbit's foot every game after that, and the Huskers did not lose for 32 straight games. It didn't stop there. He rubbed it every game through the 1970 and 1971 national championship years and his final season in 1972. After turning the job over to Osborne, Athletic Director Devaney rubbed the rabbit's foot—sometimes at halftime, if the Huskers were struggling—until his retirement. After that, I always had our lucky foot available at all the games he attended until his death.

I'm not sure what the red rabbit's foot record was, but Bob and I had a lot of fun. Nebraska SID Chris Anderson insists I bring it to games, and some of us still rub it on occasion—just in case, and in memory of Bob—and maybe that even helped Tom and Frank Solich a time or two.

Lucky Pennies

Another "Fat Fox" contribution to Nebraska football's outstanding record of success since 1962 is the Lucky Penny Collection. I've collected a great many coins since that tradition started, but not enough to change our standard of living.

Nebraska Journalism Hall of Fame sports writer Gregg McBride of the *Omaha World Herald* gets credit for starting a Husker tradition. The day before I left for New York to cover the Gotham Bowl game, I met Gregg on the street, and he said, "I just found this penny on the street. I'm not going to the game, so give it to Devaney for good luck." I did, and Nebraska beat George Mira and Miami, 36-34.

We played the penny game the next fall, and the Huskers lost only to Air Force before heading to the Orange Bowl to play Auburn. Nebraska track coach Frank Sevigne had a mile-relay team running in an Orange Bowl track meet, and he borrowed the Gotham

Bowl penny. Nebraska won the relay, but Frank had to battle through traffic to get the penny to Devaney just before the kickoff. Three plays later, quarterback Dennis Claridge ran 67 yards for a touchdown, and Nebraska won 13-7.

After that, for years I tried to find coins before every game (the Gotham Penny was retired with full honors for museum display), and fans began sending me coins in case I didn't find one. Line coach Carl Selmer took over penny duty, and I would have a packet of coins for him to carry. By the end of a season, he would have a huge package of coins packed in a pocket during games.

Serious collecting ceased when Devaney retired from coaching. And somewhere I have several coffee cans full of coins. Oh, yes, and a piece of paper play money I found it on a street in Colorado Springs before the 1965 Nebraska-Air Force game, won by Nebraska, 27-17. Whatever works—especially when your team plays better than the opponent.

Cletus's Superstition

Cletus Fischer had his own lucky coin during his coaching days as an assistant to Bill Jennings, Bob Devaney, and Tom Osborne. Clete lost a tough battle with cancer in 2000, but he left a great football legacy.

The eldest of the famed Fischer family football players, Cletus played six-man football at St. Edward, then starred at Nebraska for George "Potsy" Clark (1945), Bernie Masterson (1946-1947), and Clark again in 1948. He scored both Husker touchdowns against Notre Dame in his senior year. He coached high school teams at St. Edward (first year out of high school during WWII), Omaha South, and Midland, Texas, before joining Bill Jennings' NU staff. Clete became an outstanding offensive line coach and a key member of the Devaney and Osborne staffs before retiring.

Following Clete to Nebraska were brothers Ken (quarterback, who became a prominent Nebraska high school coach at Oakland and Grand Island); Rex (halfback, who became an obstetrician); and Pat (halfback and QB, who became a great NFL cornerback with the St. Louis Cardinals and the Washington Redskins). Clete's sons—Pat, Tim, and Dan—all earned Husker football letters. Both daughters also won letters at Nebraska; Carrie in softball and Kathleen in golf.

Cletus always dropped a nickel underneath the goal posts at Nebraska's end during pregame warm-ups. But he had to be very careful as he strolled around the warm-up area.

"I really had to watch it after the Devaney staff got here," Clete said many times. "I had to really sneak, because John Melton would watch me and then go pick up the nickel."

Melton came with Devaney from Wyoming as freshman coach and later became an outstanding linebackers coach for Bob and Tom Osborne.

Western Union Motivation

John Dervin was a starting guard on Nebraska's 1963 Big Eight and Orange Bowl championship team. He learned after the third game of the season that Coach Bob Devaney had many ways to motivate players.

Nebraska had beaten the Iowa State Cyclones, 21-7, in Lincoln, but on Monday it was announced that Iowa State's outstanding tackle, John Van Sicklin, had been named the Big Eight Defensive Player of the Week.

Before practice that afternoon, Dervin walked by the coaches' locker room, and Devaney called him in. Bob pulled out what appeared to be a Western Union telegram and said, "John, I just got this telegram, and it reads, 'Coach Devaney—Please thank John Dervin for helping me make Big Eight Defensive Player of the Week. Best regards, John Van Sicklin.'"

Dervin looked stunned for a minute and was ready to storm out cursing the Cyclone tackle, but the coaches laughed, and Bob kidded him about playing better in the rest of the games. Which he did, as the Huskers went 10-1, won the Big Eight title and beat Auburn in the Orange Bowl. Nebraska had not won a conference title since the Rose Bowl team won the Big Six in 1940. The only team to beat Nebraska in 1963 was Ben Martin's Air Force Academy. The Falcons won, 13-7, but lost a mascot. At halftime, the AF Cadets gave a demonstration with Falcons. All went well until one of the Falcons went AWOL, flying out of the stadium.

Signing Frenzy

In 1963, the National Football League and the American Football League had not merged, and competition was fierce. When the Nebraska-Auburn game ended in the Orange Bowl, scouts from both leagues charged the Husker locker room, waving contracts and pens.

Coach Devaney told me to admit them, and the scouts rushed all around the areas seeking signatures. When the steam cleared, 11 of Nebraska's 13 seniors had signed pro contracts—a great credit to former Coach Bill Jennings' recruiting and Bob Devaney and his staff's coaching.

"The Fly"

Guy "The Fly" Ingles still ranks as one of Nebraska's top split ends after starring for Bob Devaney's teams in 1968-69-70. He is fourth on the career receiving chart with 74 and third in receiving yards with 1,157.

While his receiving contributed a great deal to the success of the Huskers in their 1969 resurgence from a pair of 6-4 seasons and in nabbing a national championship in 1970, he can't shake the memory of a punt return in his sophomore season.

"We were playing Iowa State the week before the Colorado game in 1968," Ingles recalled. "I was deep, and Al Larson was the up guy. Coach Devaney had drilled us hard on me standing on the 10-yard line, and if the ball was going to go by that, I was to let it go. He also reminded us over and over to 'make sure you catch the ball.'

"While I was waiting for the punt against Iowa State, I kept telling myself, 'Please, God, don't let me drop the ball, so I have to go face Coach Devaney.' I caught the ball, but when I looked down I was straddling the goal-line, one foot in and one foot out. All I could do was run, and I got to the 12- or 15-yard line. I knew I had messed up, and when I got to the bench I hid behind five big linemen.

"All of a sudden, the big guys parted like the Red Sea, and there was Coach Devaney, with that red coat and that red hat, holding that clipboard. He looked down at me and said, 'Ingles, I thought you knew what the hell you were doing back there!'

"Later, I got another chance to field a punt right in front of our bench. Just as I caught the ball, I was hit and knocked to the ground. I was lying flat on my back, and the ball was in the air straight above me, and I knew Coach was close, but somehow the ball got kicked out of bounds to save me."

Ingles recalls a bright spot the next week against Colorado: "Out at Boulder I had a good day and took a punt back 63 yards for my first touchdown. In my senior season, I was able to catch two TD passes from Van Brownson at Boulder."

SID Pressures

Football coaches have a lot of pressure, but sports information directors take their share of abuse, too. In 1968, the Nebraska Huskers were in the midst of the second-straight 6-4 season, the low point of the Bob Devaney era. Kansas State was not held in as high esteem as it is these days under Bill Snyder, and Devaney's Huskers were losing 12-0 to the Wildcats on Homecoming. A shut-out loss to K-State on Homecoming was a bitter pill for Bob to swallow, and it was really tough for the fans to handle. Walking down through the Memorial Stadium crowd on my way to coordinate the postgame media interviews, a West Stadium fan yelled, "Bryant, you SOB, how are you going to explain this damn thing away?"

The Darkest Day

November 22, 1963 was a terrible day in the history of our country. President John F. Kennedy was assassinated in Dallas, and America was shocked into deep mourning.

Volney Meece, longtime sportswriter at the *Oklahoma City Times* and the *Daily Oklahoman,* as well as secretary of the Football Writers Association of America for years, and I were eating lunch in Barry's Bar across the street from the *Lincoln Journal and Star* Building when we heard the news.

A man opened the door and yelled, "The President has been shot!" Volney and I immediately ran across the street to the newsroom and followed the story on the *Associated Press* wire until it was announced that the President was dead. It was the beginning of a long day and night and a trying Saturday.

Volney was in town to cover the Nebraska-Oklahoma football game the next day, but the President's death put an immediate pall on the game. We went to the University of Nebraska Coliseum, where a decision about playing the game would be made.

Among the decision makers were Nebraska AD Tippy Dye, football coaches Bob Devaney of Nebraska and Bud Wilkinson of Oklahoma, Big Eight Commissioner Wayne Duke, and several concerned representatives of the Orange Bowl Committee.

OU and the Huskers were scheduled to play for the conference championship and a spot in the Orange Bowl, but games were being canceled all over the country in the wake of the tragedy.

There were long hours of deliberations, and it was not until late on Friday night that a decision was made to play the game. Wayne Duke contacted the NCAA and other conference schools, and the administrators of both schools were involved in the process. Other conferences were contacted, also. It wasn't decided to play the game until after Bud Wilkinson managed to contact Bobby Kennedy, the President's brother. Wilkinson was the director of the President's Council on Physical Fitness, and he reported that Bobby Kennedy urged the game to be played because "the President would want you to play." At that point, there was a "go" to play three Big Eight games, primarily because of Bud's phone call. But they did not happen.

Late Saturday morning when hushed fans were gathering at Memorial Stadium, Nebraska learned that the other conference schools had decided to cancel, leaving Nebraska and Oklahoma open to considerable criticism across the country. A pregame service and tribute to President Kennedy was held, and the Huskers managed a 29-20 win for Bob Devaney's first conference title in Bud Wilkinson's last game at OU. But it was bittersweet.

Auld Lang Syne

Even the best laid plans don't always work out, despite repeated attempts to guarantee communications. Bob Devaney's last Big Eight game was on November 23, 1972—nine years to the day since he had won his first championship by defeating Oklahoma the day after President Kennedy had been assassinated.

Once again, the opponent was Oklahoma, and athletic staff members were anxious to do something special to mark his retirement. We arranged to have the Cornhusker Marching Band play "Auld Lang Syne" as the game was ending—assuming of course the Cornhuskers would defeat the Sooners. Devaney had a very good team, led by Heisman Trophy winner Johnny Rodgers and Outland-Lombardi winner Rich Glover, so there was reason to be optimistic.

Not so fast, Fox! Rodgers had a touchdown reception nullified when he was forced out of bounds, then came back on the field to catch the ball and score. As the final seconds ticked off the clock, it was apparent the Sooners were going to win, 17-14, and the "Auld Lang Syne" salute somehow seemed inappropriate.

I ran down the East sideline track, hollering at the band, "Don't play 'Auld Lang Syne'!" They didn't hear me, and as the game ended, the song wafted over Memorial Stadium. However, neither Devaney nor anyone else realized why or for what reason.

Ironically, it was later determined that Oklahoma had used an ineligible player, and the Sooners forfeited the game, giving Nebraska its eighth conference title in Devaney's 11 years. However, the Nebraska record book still carries that game as a Sooner victory. "Auld Lang Syne," that is!

Weir Lauds Rockne

Ed Weir was Nebraska's first two-time All-America selection, and he had a life-long appreciation of his relationship with Notre Dame legend Knute Rockne.

Weir, who retired after an illustrious career as Nebraska's long-time track coach, also had great respect for Cornhusker football coach Bob Devaney. Prior to the Nebraska-Notre Dame game in the 1973 Orange Bowl, Weir was a favorite source for the media about his days playing against Rockne's Irish. *The Lincoln Star* reported Weir's appraisal of both coaches: "He

(Rockne) was a great coach, a fellow the players—his and the opponents—really liked and respected. He was a helluva guy. I've been to coaching schools with him, and he was great to me. He was tops. Actually, Bob Devaney comes as close to duplicating Rockne as any coach I've known—his personality, on and off the field, and the way he carries the respect of his own players and that of his opponents."

3
Osborne

Tom Osborne—
Dr., Coach, Congressman

Travel roster expansions were not the only things
that would amaze the world of college football as the
new century opened. College football players not only
attended college on scholarships that paid thousands
of dollars enroute to their graduations, the outstanding
players often left the classrooms after their sophomore
or junior seasons to join the NFL—thanks to millions
of dollars in bonus enticements.

Even Nebraska's legendary football coach, Tom
Osborne, wearied of retirement leisure and surprised
the fans by deciding to run for the United States Con-
gress from the Third District of Nebraska! But it was
no surprise when Dr. Osborne, a Nebraska icon with a
Hall of Fame plaque and three national football championships on his resume, galloped through Western

Nebraska to a GOP seat in the House of Representatives.

Few Nebraskans have ever received the respect and admiration extended Tom Osborne, whose Husker football teams capped a 25-year career with a five-year finale of 60 wins, only three losses and a trio of national titles.

Osborne is Husker History

Check one of Chris Anderson's Nebraska football media guides, and you get the picture of what an impact Bob Devaney and Tom Osborne made on Husker history—and big shoes passed on to Tom's successor, Frank Solich: No. 1 national ranking by winning percentage (1962-1997); five national championships; 18 bowl victories; 21 conference titles; 26 first-round NFL selections; 28 Top 10 rankings; 33 nine-win seasons; 34 bowl trips; 36 consecutive winning seasons; 44 Academic All-America players; 64 All-America players; 227 sold-out games at Memorial Stadium; 356 wins; two Heisman Trophy winners; eight Outlands, four Lombardis, a Butkus Award, and a Johnny Unitas Golden Arm Award. A remarkable record for two Hall of Fame coaches who became the third pair of Division 1 coaches to post successive 100-wins—and they were the first to do it in only 21 years.

"Can I Come Too?"

Bowl games frequently produced interesting events during the Devaney-Osborne eras. Several days before the 1974 Cotton Bowl game with Texas, Coach Tom Osborne ordered a curfew and started holding bed check. At a staff meeting the morning after Tom and Trainer George Sullivan made the rounds at 11 p.m., the Husker coach broke the staff up with his experience.

Tom Ruud and Bob Nelson, a pair of outstanding linebackers who would go on to NFL careers, roomed together and were tucked in for the night when Coach Osborne came to visit. While Tom was surveying the room, the patio door curtains parted, and a voice said, "C'mon guys, the coast is clear."

"I turned on the light and there was Maury Damkroger (senior fullback) and I said, 'Can I come along, too, Maury?' " Osborne recounted. Sullivan reported rapidly retreating footsteps heading back toward Maury's room. Nelson logged 11 years in the NFL, including three with the Buffalo Bills, seven with the Oakland Raiders and one with the Seattle Seahawks. Ruud played three years with the Bills and two with the Cincinnati Bengals, while Damkroger played two years with the New England Patriots.

All three were provided extra conditioning opportunities in preparation for the Cotton Bowl game with Texas. It helped pay off with a 19-3 win over the Longhorns.

In 2001, Ruud's son Barrett became a solid linebacker in his freshman season at Nebraska.

A Royal Act

Nebraska's visit to the Cotton Bowl to play the Texas Longhorns provided a memory of outstanding sportsmanship displayed by one of the good old boys of college football, Coach Darrell Royal.

Nebraska had won the game, 19-3, and most coaches would choose to lick their wounds in private. Not Royal, who had played quarterback at Oklahoma before launching his coaching career. Husker coach Tom Osborne was busy with TV crews outside the locker room where I was guarding the door.

Darrell came to the door and said, "Don, I'd like to say a few words to your team. Is that OK?" I assured him it was, arranged for a bench for him to talk from, and notified the assistant coaches before introducing the Texas coach.

A hushed NU team heard the future Hall of Fame coach say, "I just want you men to know what an honor it was for the University of Texas team to play you in the Cotton Bowl. We congratulate you for the great game you played, and I want to wish all of you the best of luck in all that you do in the future."

It was a class act, and Darrell left with Cornhusker cheers ringing in his ears.

The Hunt for No. 1

One of the wonderful things about college football is fan support for their favorite team. Every school has die-hard students and alumni who love the team—win, lose or tie—but preferably win.

Nebraska lost only one game in 1982, a 27-24 decision at Penn State. Joe Paterno's team went on to win the national championship, and Nebraska wound up

No. 3 with a 12-1 record, including an Orange Bowl win over Louisiana State.

Huskers fans have always claimed Penn State had an odd-shaped football field that enabled the Nittany Lions to win the game by catching passes out of bounds. Penn State had beaten the Huskers, 30-24, the year before, and Nebraska had won, 21-7, in 1980 at State College. NU also won, 42-17, at Lincoln in 1979, so a colorful four-game series between two class programs led by two class coaches, Paterno and Osborne, wound up 2-2.

At the NCAA convention following the 1982 season, I visited with Joe and sincerely congratulated him on winning the national title. One of the real good guys in coaching, he grinned and said, "Thanks a lot, Don, and we both know how we won it."

Both of us knew—and still know—you have to be good to win a national championship, but you also have to have a little luck along the way. Nebraska fans who were still upset about the loss at Penn State in 1982 really enjoyed the 1983 Kickoff Classic game at Giants Stadium in the Meadowlands. The Huskers beat Penn State 44-6 to open the season and won 12 straight games before losing 31-30 to Miami in the Orange Bowl. Nebraska needed luck at Penn State and luck in the Orange Bowl when the Huskers went for two to win in the final minute, only to misfire by inches.

Such is life in the hunt for No. 1.

Reverence for the Bear

When Alabama came to Lincoln in 1977, the Tide was ranked No. 4 in the nation. Tom Osborne was in his fifth season since succeeding Bob Devaney, and the Cornhuskers were upset by Washington State in the opener, 19-10.

Nebraska dropped from 15th to being unranked with Bear Bryant and Alabama up next. It was Bryant's turn to be upset, as the Huskers beat the Tide, 31-24.

Bear Bryant

Most memorable: the reverence for Coach Bryant demonstrated by Husker players and fans. When the gun sounded, Nebraska players raced to Bear and clamored to shake his hand. I escorted him through a tunnel of fans trying to shake his hand to the Tide locker room as the Husker fans yelled best wishes and good luck to him. A few days later, I received a letter from Coach Bryant in which he expressed thanks and commended the Nebraska team for its outstanding play. He also wrote "the treatment we received from the Nebraska fans was the finest any of my teams have received anywhere."

Oklahoma OB Replay

Warren Powers didn't stop with upsetting Nebraska in 1977. His Washington State team's 19-10 win at Lincoln launched a fierce rivalry between the former Nebraska (and Oakland Raiders) player and his former boss, Tom Osborne. Powers was wooed away from Washington State after just one season by the University of Missouri of the Big Eight.

Powers and Osborne had a tiff of sorts prior to the 1977 season, when Warren departed Nebraska for his first head coaching job. Osborne wanted to exchange film of each team's spring football game, but Powers chose not to honor the idea. Not surprising, since he knew everything about Nebraska and Osborne knew very little about Washington State's season-opening prospects under new coach Warren Powers.

Former Nebraska player and assistant coach Warren Powers chats with his ex-boss, Tom Osborne.

After moving to Missouri, Powers added injury to insult in 1978. On Veterans Day, Osborne's No. 4 team upset No. 1-ranked Oklahoma, 17-14, thanks to Jeff Hansen's jarring tackle of Billy Sims that caused a game-saving fumble recovered by Jim Pillen. All that remained for Nebraska to win the Big Eight and make a bid for the national title was to beat unranked Missouri at home the next week.

Not so fast, as they say. No. 2 Nebraska once again fell victim to the former Husker assistant coach. Missouri knocked off the Cornhuskers, 35-31, and caused more damage to Tom Osborne and his team than anyone could have imagined. Instead of going to the Orange Bowl and playing for the national championship, the Huskers had to go to the Orange Bowl and play Oklahoma again!

The 1978 Orange Bowl replay game was a bitter pill for Coach Tom Osborne and the Cornhuskers. Nebraska, under Osborne, had lost five straight to the Oklahoma Sooners, and the shocking upset of No. 1 Oklahoma sent waves of euphoria across the Memorial Stadium crowd and the state. Fans could start thinking of Tom as a worthy successor to Bob Devaney. Likewise, the media.

Following the NU loss to Mizzou, the Orange Bowl delegation, all friends of long standing, came into the Nebraska locker room area and asked my assistance in finding a telephone. I took them to Glen Abbott's equipment room near the locker room, and a call was placed to Orange Bowl Miami headquarters. No secret, they were checking to see what team would be invited to the Orange Bowl to play Big Eight co-champion Nebraska.

The caller hung up the phone, turned to me and said, "Fox, you won't believe this, and I'm sorry—it's Oklahoma!" Somewhat stunned, I said, "You've got to be kidding!" But he wasn't.

The OB Committee prided itself on matching the two highest-ranked teams, and co-champion Oklahoma was the highest- ranked team available. The delegation then said, "Fox, you've got to take us to Tom so we can break the bad news." We moved into the locker room and found Osborne, dejected by the loss to Missouri, and he received the news with the enthusiasm of an innocent man getting a death sentence.

Like everyone else, he said, "You can't be serious—that's a terrible decision." The OB delegation offered condolences and assured Tom they would do all in their power to provide the Nebraska team a good time in Miami.

Tom assured them that he, his staff, and the team would play the game and do what they had to do in Miami, but stressed, "We're not happy about this whole replay idea. We shouldn't have to play a team we've already beaten."

Oklahoma won the Orange Bowl replay game, 31-24, and Osborne, his staff, the players, and fans did not enjoy that trip to Miami.

Ironically, Warren Powers lost his next six games with Nebraska before being replaced by Woody Woodenhofer, and the Missouri Tigers have not beaten Nebraska since that 1978 upset, a string of 22 straight Husker wins.

Osborne's Record

The University of Nebraska has had six football coaches enshrined in the National Football Foundation's College Football Hall of Fame.

Dr. Tom Osborne, now United States Congressman from the Third District of Nebraska, is the only one to march directly from Tom Osborne Field into the Hall of Fame. The National Football Foundation

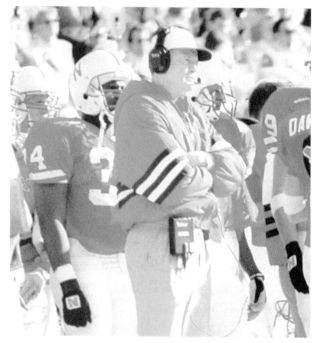

Husker Coach Tom Osborne

waived the usual waiting period for Hall of Fame inductions and elected Tom to membership when he retired in 1998.

Recognizing Osborne's unprecedented record in his final five years, his service to intercollegiate football during his entire 25-year career, as well as to youth, his community, state, and nation, the Foundation moved fast.

Osborne's final five-year record may be hard for any coach to duplicate. During the 1993-1997 span, his teams won 60 games and lost only three. The Huskers had three undefeated seasons, won three national titles, four conference championships, and four bowl games. His career record was 255-49-3, and his winning percentage of .836 trailed only Knute Rockne (.881) and Frank Leahy (.864) of Notre Dame, George Woodruff (.846) of Penn, Illinois, and Yale, and Barry Switzer of Oklahoma (.837).

Only Bear Bryant (323), who coached at Maryland, Kentucky, Texas A&M, and Alabama; Joe Paterno (317) of Penn State, and Bobby Bowden (304) of Florida State had logged more victories among Division I-A schools heading into the 2000 football season.

Nebraska's other Hall of Fame coaches are Fielding Yost (1898), elected in 1951; Dana X. Bible (1929-36), elected in 1951; Lawrence "Biff" Jones (1937-41), elected in 1954; E.N. Robinson (1896-97), elected in 1955; and Bob Devaney (1962-1972), elected in 1981.

Cornhuskers in Japan

Nebraska and Kansas State moved their football game from Manhattan, Kansas, to Tokyo. Both teams flew together on the same plane from Kansas City to Vancouver, B.C. to Tokyo in December, 1992.

In Tokyo, the game was billed as the Coca-Cola Bowl, with No. 11-ranked Nebraska the visiting team meeting unranked Kansas State, the home team. It was a cultural experience for all concerned, but the game and the surrounding atmosphere were different. Fans were seated far from the playing field in the indoor arena, and loud rock music blared throughout the game, won by the Huskers, 38-24. Each team had been "adopted" by a Japanese city, and their citizens comprised cheering sections.

The Cornhuskers had a much more prominent reputation in Tokyo than Kansas State, and it was evident the hosts were somewhat more attentive to Coach Tom Osborne than the Wildcats and Coach Bill Snyder. Bill is one of the top football coaches in the profession, and he has done a tremendous job with the Kansas State program for a long time. But I know he did not enjoy the trip to Tokyo.

A lasting memory of Tokyo developed the afternoon that associate athletic director Al Papik, assistant AD Joe Selig and I toured Tokyo on the rail system that circles the city. We wound up in a station and could not decide what track we should take to our next stop. Unable to read Japanese, we obviously appeared puzzled looking up at signs.

A young woman approached and asked if we were lost. We told her we were, and she told us what gate to take. Grateful, I told her we were with the Nebraska football team and gave her a Cornhusker booster pin. "Oh," she said, smiling. "I know Nebraska—I belong to Mutual of Omaha!"

An Unhappy Upset

Nebraska football teams under Bob Devaney and Tom Osborne seldom self-destructed, so the 1986 Fiesta Bowl game was an exception. But it was a real beauty, or a real ugly if you were a Cornhusker.

Tom Osborne's No. 7-ranked Huskers took a 9-2 record to Tempe for a New Year's date with No. 5 Michigan, and at halftime the Huskers appeared to be heading for a romp. That didn't happen.

Two Doug DuBose touchdowns in the second quarter overcame a 3-0 Wolverine first-quarter lead, and Nebraska seemed to be in command. Then came one of the quickest turnarounds in memory. In 13 minutes, Michigan went from 14-3 down to 27-14 up, and the Huskers could muster only nine points in the final quarter to lose, 27-23.

Later, Michigan coach Bo Schembechler said, "At halftime, my coaching staff and I were stunned. No team had dominated us like Nebraska did in that first half. We were wondering what we could do to get back in the game."

Nebraska had the unexpected solution. On the third play after the second-half kickoff, the Huskers fumbled at their 21-yard line, and a Gerald White touchdown made it a 14-10 game. On the second play after the ensuing kickoff, Nebaska fumbled again, and Jim Harbaugh scored a touchdown to put the Wolverines ahead, 17-14. Next, Michigan blocked a Dan Wingard punt at the NU six-yard line, but the Husker Black Shirts stiffened and allowed only a field goal. Finally, after two NU interception penalties, Harbaugh again plunged over for a touchdown to bring the third quarter to an end. Nebraska got a TD and a safety in the final quarter, but the 24-point Wolverine third-quarter bonanza was too much to overcome.

Tittle Remembers Osborne

One of the most enjoyable and prestigious sports events is the annual Walter Camp Foundation banquet in New Haven, Connecticut, which honors its All-America football team.

I attended the affair for some 20 years and served on the Camp Foundation board for several years. The New Haven hospitality and the enthusiasm of the Foundation members is outstanding. College All-Americans rate the Walter Camp tops among the all-star salutes, and many have returned year after year to enjoy the banquet and assist in the fund-raising projects.

In 1989, Y.A. Tittle, famed quarterback of the San Francisco 49ers and the New York Giants, received the Walter Camp Distinguished American Award at the banquet. After the dinner, Tittle told me a story:

"You know, I was a teammate of that Tom Osborne of yours. Only I didn't realize it for a long time. I watched the guy coach on the sidelines, and I liked the way he acted. I also liked the things he said. But it never dawned on me that I knew the guy," Y.A. said.

"One day a former teammate said, 'You know that guy—he was on the 49ers with you,' and I said, 'You mean that skinny kid we had as a receiver?' And sure enough it was, but he had put on a lot more weight than when he was on our team."

Tittle added, "The thing I remember about that skinny kid was how hard he worked. He wasn't real fast, but he worked like the devil all the time."

That's the Tom Osborne Nebraska football fans have known for a long time.

The "Roosky" Plays

Nebraska went one-for-two on scoring "Roosky" plays during the first 11 years of the Tom Osborne era. Tom first called the "Bummeroosky Play" against Missouri in 1975 with 1:46 left in the first half at Columbia. The Cornhuskers lined up to punt, but the snap went to fullback Tony Davis, who pushed the ball through John O'Leary's legs and then turned and faked the ball to Monte Anthony running toward the right. All the Nebraska players ran right also, while O'Leary stood still for a couple seconds as the Tigers chased Anthony, then O'Leary ran around left end 40 yards to score. That paved the way for a 30-7 Husker victory.

Against Oklahoma in 1979 at Norman, Osborne unveiled the "Fumbleroosky Play" in an effort to catch the Sooners. Quarterback Jeff Quinn took a snap and immediately laid the ball on the ground by his foot and faked a run to the right.

All-America guard Randy Schleusener scooped up the ball and ran around left end 15 yards for a touchdown with 4:43 left in the game. It wasn't enough. Oklahoma won, 17-14.

Bernie Kosar's two touchdown passes and a Jeff Davis field goal gave Miami a first-quarter jump, 17-0. But once again, Tom Osborne dusted off The Fumbleroosky. This time, Quarterback Turner Gill set the snap by his foot. Enter All-America guard Dean Steinkuhler—the Outland-Lombardi winner—who grabbed up the ball and galloped around left end 19 yards to score.

The Huskers outscored Miami, 16-14, in the second half, but the Hurricanes gained the national championship on the failed two-point play as the game ended.

Neither the "Fumbleroosky" or the "Bummeroosky" reside any longer in the Cornhusker playbook, by the way.

The Number Switcheroo

Sending Dean Steinkuhler on a touchdown run with a deliberately "fumbled" football wasn't the only trick pulled out of the Osborne bag in the 1984 Orange Bowl game.

Husker secondary coaches attempted to confuse the Miami offense by having two defensive backs switch jersey numbers for the game.

Senior monster back Mike McCashland had always worn No. 2, while senior cornerback Dave Burke

had always worn No. 33. But they swapped jerseys for the Hurricanes. It can be noted that Steinkuhler's Fumbleroosky worked better than the McCashland-Burke jersey switch. Bernie Kosar hit two touchdown passes in the first quarter as Miami sprinted in front, 17-0.

The biggest confusion caused by the jersey switch occurred in the Orange Bowl press box and the network television booth. One of Kosar's passes was picked off by No. 2, and everyone thought Mike McCashland had the interception. But "No. 2" was really Dave Burke, who should have been wearing No. 33, which was being worn by McCashland.

4

Husker Heroes

Gone Too Soon

One of the most tragic events in Nebraska football history came in the spring of 1996 when Brook Berringer was killed in a private plane crash.

Brook had backed up Tommie Frazier and played key roles as a starter when Frazier was laid low by blood clots.

Both shared in the glory as Nebraska beat Miami, 24-17, in the 1995 Orange Bowl to present Coach Tom Osborne with his first of three national championships. Berringer led the Huskers in passing with eight completions for 81 yards and threw a touchdown pass to Mark Gilman after Miami had taken a 10-0 lead in the first quarter.

News of Brook's death sent shock waves across Nebraska, and thousands of Husker fans mourned the young man who had contributed to Nebraska's success on the football field and also had devoted a great deal of his time to youth activities and community service.

On the morning after the plane crash that killed Brook, my long-time secretary Janette Sojka arrived at the South Stadium office building and found a bouquet of flowers, with a card that read, "Thanks, Brook! You were special! Your loving fan" leaning against the front door.

The card was attached to a piece of ruled notebook paper on which was printed this tribute: "May you be lifted up by angels . . . To soar upon wings of an eagle . . . And touch the face of God. God bless you on your journey #18 . . . We love you, Brook! The People of Nebraska."

Setting the Record Straight

One of the annual events that helped make life in the fast lane of college athletics interesting and enjoyable for me was the annual NCAA Convention. Athletic directors, faculty representatives, coaches, various administrators, the media, and commercial exhibitors would gather at a large hotel in different cities for several days in January. The purpose was to consider new NCAA legislation that would assist in the proper administration of intercollegiate athletics.

Prior to college presidents assuming full command of college athletics, the faculty representatives did the voting, while athletic directors and other administrators were admitted to sessions as alternate delegates or visiting delegates. In recent years, college presidents and a board of directors system has made decisions, with faculty representatives and athletic directors providing consultation. During my 30-year NCAA run, the best part of the conventions was the renewal of friendships with delegates and the media from all parts of the country. It was like a fraternity reunion, lots of camaraderie, gab sessions, political posturing, emotional speeches, and angry rebuttals. Well, yes, like a national political convention to nominate a presidential candidate.

Only delegates and alternates were permitted to address the convention business sessions. I usually had an alternate badge, but I only went to a floor microphone once. It was in the late 1970s, and a floor battle was taking place about some issue I cannot recall, because the oratory was less than admirable. A delegate gave a fiery address and included a statement such as, "We have reached a point where we have a player named I.M. Hipp walk-on from Alabama to Nebraska, and that shouldn't happen," or words to that effect.

Becoming wide awake on that, I went to the microphone and called, "Mr. President, Don Bryant from the University of Nebraska," and was recognized by the Chair. In my best political convention voice, the hall filled with, "Mr. President, I rise for a point of order to ask that the record of this convention show that Isaiah

Moses Hipp walked on at the University of Nebraska from the Great State of South Carolina, not Alabama!"

A standing ovation filled the room on my return march to obscurity in the hallowed world of NCAA legislative action. Better known as I.M. Hipp, the player in question lettered for Tom Osborne teams in 1977-78-79, earning All-Big 8 honors as a sophomore. He ranks No. 5 on the all-time rushing list with 2,814 yards, 14 games over 100 yards and 21 touchdowns. The Chapin, S.C., star was inducted into the Nebraska Football Hall of Fame in 1995.

"We're GOING to Win it"

Dan Jenkins, a distinguished sports writer and novelist, received the coveted Jake Wade Award from the College Sports Information Directors Association in 1999. Dan is an old friend from his *Sports Illustrated* days, who continues to write books and is a veteran on the *Golf Digest* staff.

He gained universal acclaim for his football stories during a 23-year career with *Sports Illustrated*. An alumnus of Texas Christian University, Dan's novel, *Semi-Tough* was a best-seller and a classic Burt Reynolds movie. In 1972, Nebraska All-America wingback Johnny Rodgers was a top candidate for the Heisman Trophy, and I've always credited Jenkins with pushing him over the top.

Dan located me the week of the Nebraska-Colorado game in Denver, where I was stranded in a hotel room by a huge snowstorm. He said, "Get together all you can on Johnny for me, and if he has a good day, I'm ready to push him for the Heisman." I called my top assistant, Tom "Mini-Fox" Simons, who prepared massive information for Dan. Rodgers had a great day, including a dazzling punt return against the Buffs, and Dan's report in *SI* endorsed Johnny as the front-runner for the Heisman.

During a reunion at the CoSIDA luncheon in 1999, Dan told me, "Johnny was really something to watch," and recalled a special memory about the 1971 Nebraska-Oklahoma "Game of the Century" game at Norman.

"I remember coming to Nebraska, and you lining up interviews with players for me; then I went to Oklahoma, and John Keith arranged for me to talk to the Sooner players," Dan said. "The thing I remember most was the way all the Nebraska players said, 'We're going to win the game—somehow we'll find a way to win it!' All the OU players kept saying, 'We've got a chance to win it.' "

That's what happened: Oklahoma had a chance to win the game, and Nebraska found a way to win it, 35-31. Johnny Rodgers' unforgettable punt return early and his diving third-down reception of a Jerry Tagge pass for a first down kept the Huskers' final victory march alive.

Two Men to Revere

Rich Glover and Doug Dumler were two outstanding players on the 1971 national championship Nebraska team. Dumler was an All-America center, while Glover was a two-time All-America middle guard who would win the Outland Trophy and the Lombardi Awards as the nation's top lineman in 1972. After watching a Husker scrimmage in 1971 and enjoying a heated battle between the two teammates. I recalled an old Russian song, "Abdul El Bul-Bul Amir and Ivan Skizavitsky Skivar." I took the liberty of writing new lyrics. With apologies to the Russians and the songwriter, my version went like this:

The sons of Nebraska are hardy and bold,
And quite unaccustomed to fear.
But the bravest of all is a man, so it's told,
Named Glover—a man to revere.

If they want a pass rush of magnificent force,
Or to capture a back from the rear,
Or to storm roundabout, Devaney will shout,
For Glover—a man to revere.

There are heroes in plenty and men known to fame,
Who play on Nebraska's green "rug."
But none of more fame than a man by the name
Of Dumler—a center called Doug.

He can sing like Caruso, both tenor and bass,
Or handle his dukes like a pug.
He is quite the cream of the Cornhusker team,
Mr. Dumler—a center called Doug.

One day this bold center entered the fray,
And bent over the ball with a sneer.
He was looking for fun when he happened to run
Into Glover—a man to revere.

"Young man," said Glover, "Is existence so dull,
That you're anxious to end your career?
For center, you know, you've trod on the toe
Of Glover—a man to revere."

"So take your last look at the sunshine and brook,
You're about to recline on our 'rug.'
By which, I imply, you are going to die,
Mr. Dumler—a center called Doug."

"Not so, Mr. Glover—a man to revere,"
Replied Dumler—a center called Doug.
"You may be most quick and mighty good with a
trick,
But I'll block you with one mighty shrug."

They fought through the fight by sunshine so bright,
The battle was heard far and near.
But when Bob stopped the fun—they were both No.
1, Two Cornhuskers that all can revere.

Lloyd Grimm

During 2000, Lloyd Grimm, former University of Nebraska football and basketball star, passed away at age 83. He was a former U.S. Marshal who had been confined to a wheelchair from wounds he received from a Native American sniper during the Wounded Knee siege on the Pine Ridge Reservation in South Dakota.

Following his athletic career at Nebraska (1937-38), Lloyd served as a U.S. Navy pilot during World War II. News of his death in Omaha brought back memories to two of his former teammates.

Elmer Dohrmann, Nebraska's all-time letter winner, recalled Grimm's toughness. "He was really a tough, physical player," Dohrmann said. "He played end with me, and he was very aggressive. He was really tough on defense, a hard charger who ripped through the offense." Dohrmann won 11 Cornhusker letters, three in football, basketball, and baseball, and two in track between 1935 and 1937.

Paul Amen, who played the opposite end from Dohrmann and Grimm, earned three letters in football, basketball, and baseball during the same period, also remembered Lloyd's basketball prowess. "He also played basketball the way he played football, tough and physical," Amen said. "We were running a play and switching on a screen. Lloyd went all out on a switch, but he collided with one of our guys and flattened him." Amen was an assistant football coach on Earl Blaik's famed Army teams during World War II and also served as head baseball coach at the U.S. Military Academy. He later became head football coach at Wake Forest before becoming a banker. Both Amen and Dohrmann have been enshrined in the Nebraska Football and Basketball Halls of Fame.

Spectacular Johnny Rodgers

Johnny Rodgers is the only Nebraska player I've watched who caused the fans to get ready to stand up whenever he ran on the field. Johnny could do it all—run, catch, pass, and could have no doubt punted in an emergency.

The Heisman Trophy winner in 1972, sweeping every area of the nation in the voting, was a two-time All-America wingback for Bob Devaney. His sensational pass receiving and dazzling punt returns contributed a great deal to Nebraska's national championship runs in 1970 and 1971.

Against Notre Dame in the 1973 Orange Bowl game, his final Husker appearance after winning the Heisman in December, Johnny paraded his talents by starting at I-back for the first time and leading the Huskers in rushing with 81 yards. More spectacular, the Omaha native scored three touchdowns rushing, threw a 52-yard TD pass to Frosty Anderson, and caught a 50-yard scoring pass from Dave Humm in the 40-6 rout of the Irish.

Five touchdowns—running, throwing and catching—provided on-the-field-fireworks as a colorful ending to an impressive college career. Johnny Rodgers might have made All-Big Eight, if Bob Devaney had asked him to play left guard, right cornerback or middle linebacker. Johnny was inducted into the National Football Hall of Fame in 2000.

'Trainwreck'

They're have been a lot of outstanding and tough football players, but one stands far above the rest. Tom Novak, a bruising back out of Omaha South High School, still is the toughest human being I've ever known. "Trainwreck," as he was known during his University of Nebraska career, is the only player ever to earn All-Conference honors four consecutive years.

Tom was the All-Big Six fullback in 1946, following Navy service during the war, and was the All-Conference center his final three years. His technique as a linebacker was simple: Have no regard for your body and get to the ball carrier. Notre Dame whipped Nebraska, 31-0, at South Bend in 1947, and the Irish voted Novak on their All-Opponent team for his ferocious play in a losing battle.

While jerseys have been retired for Nebraska players who have won top national honors (Heisman, Outland, Lombardi, for example), only No. 60 has not been worn since 1949 and will never again be worn by a

Husker football player. Following the season that year, Tom Novak's peers—the members of the N-Club letter-winners organization —voted unanimously to retire Tom Novak's number for all-time.

Trainwreck spent the last 25 years of his life as a paraplegic after a fall left him paralyzed from the neck down. But he accepted that challenge with the same toughness and determination he always exhibited on the football field. His courage those last years was an inspiration to all who knew him.

Each fall since 1950, the University of Nebraska presents the Tom Novak Trophy, sponsored by the late J. Gordon Roberts and Roberts Dairy, to the "Husker senior who best exemplifies courage and determination despite all odds in the manner of Nebraska All-America center Tom Novak."

Tom Novak gained renown in professional wrestling, as well as in football and baseball at the University of Nebraska. "Trainwreck" worked for years as a referee for Omaha promoter Joe Dusek and Lincoln promoter Jack Pesek, a football teammate who held the Husker season punting average record from 1947 until 1990, when Mike Stigge bumped Jack's mark of 41.2 with 41.4.

During the 1950s, I moonlighted as the ring announcer for Pesek's grapple cards at Lincoln's Pershing Auditorium. Those were the days of Dr. X , Dick the Bruiser, Hans Schmidt, Kinji Shibuya, Mitsu Arakawa, the midget star Sky Low Low, Ernie Dusek, and Verne

Gagne, a former Minnesota football player and wrestler who played against Novak and Pesek during their playing days.

Whenever I climbed into the ring to announce the card, the National Anthem, or the officials in attendance at ringside, Novak would say something to crack me up. I introduced him as "one of the all-time great Cornhuskers, Tom 'Trainwreck' Novak," and the fans would boo. When the National Anthem record started spinning, Tom liked to point out fans at ringside who had heckled him in past events. One night during the Anthem, Tom whispered, "See that fat gal on the front row to the right? Last week, she stuck me in the rear end with her hat pin."

Novak always accused Pesek of protecting his punting record by refusing to kick short "poochers." "Whenever we had to punt short, Jack would holler for Jim 'Squat' Myers to come in to punt," Tom needled.

Tom Novak was a regular on Gerry Rosenberger's fishing expedition to Lake Vermilion in Minnesota. "Rosie" hosted athletic department staff members, friends, and media at his home on Pine Island, one of the largest islands in the huge lake.

In keeping with his reputation for having "no regard for his body," Tom wore only swimming trunks when everyone else bundled up in parkas and rain gear to combat the bitter cold and icy water. One day Gerry asked Tom to bring in some wood for the fireplace, a simple request to go out to the wood pile and carry in some small logs.

About half an hour later, we heard someone yelling, "Help, Help!" and we discovered Novak, barefoot and wearing swim trunks, dragging a 30-foot birch tree on his bleeding shoulder into the yard.

Rosie explained he only wanted a couple of small logs, and Tom responded, "You asked for some wood, and I got you some wood—get me an ax, and I'll chop the tree up!"

All-America Works of Art

The University of Nebraska football program has developed 84 players who received All-America honors since the school's first season in 1890. It took 25 years before Walter Camp located Nebraska. Most All-American players selected by Camp and others played east of the Mississippi River, with heavy emphasis on the East Coast teams.

Ironically, Nebraska's first All-America player was named by Camp a year after he played his final season. Vic Halligan was honored on the 1915 Walter Camp team, but 1914 was his last year as a Cornhusker.

Beautiful oil paintings of all 84 Nebraska All-America players are on display in the South Memorial Stadium office building. Paintings of national special award winners are also on display in the All-America tunnel. That collection includes: Outland Trophy—

Larry Jacobson (1971), Rich Glover (1972), Dave Rimington (1981-1982), Dean Steinkuhler (1983), Will Shields (1992), Zach Wiegert (1995). Heisman Trophy: Johnny Rodgers (1972) and Mike Rozier (1983). Lombardi Award: Rich Glover (1972), Dave Rimington (1982), Dean Steinkuhler (1983), and Grant Wistrom (1997). Dick Butkus Award—Trev Alberts (1993). Johnny Unitas Golden Arm Award: Tommie Frazier (1995).

The Cornhusker All-America football oil paintings are signed "T. McDonald." That name may be familiar to long-time Nebraska and Philadelphia Eagles fans. He's Tommy McDonald, who came out of Albuquerque, New Mexico, to become an All-America halfback for Bud Wilkinson at the University of Oklahoma. After helping lead the Sooners to the 1956 National Championship, Tommy became a great receiver and star for the Eagles. McDonald teamed with Clendon Thomas to form one of the outstanding backfield tandem in college history. Tommy now operates his athletic portrait business in King of Prussia, Pennsylvania.

Write-In Vote

When Omaha banker Jim Fitl discovered a 1950 copy of *Look* magazine while checking his memorabilia stacks, he rushed it off to me in 1999. The magazine carried Grantland Rice's All-America football team, selected by the members of the Football Writers Association of America. Some 489 FWAA members, including me, sent in ballots to Rice that fall and were listed in the magazine. I confess to fudging a bit, since I had been recalled to active duty by the Marine Corps for the Korean War. As a result, I only saw three games before reporting with reserve fighter squadron VMF-113, but I managed to send in a ballot with a vote for Husker sophomore sensation Bobby Reynolds, now in the College Football Hall of Fame.

Other Nebraska voters in 1950 were Fred Ware and Gregg McBride of the *Omaha World Herald*; Walter Dobbins and Dick Becker of the *Nebraska State (Lincoln) Journal*; and Norris Anderson and George Miller of *The Lincoln Star*.

Heroic Buck Barger

It's been a long time since World War II ended, but Nebraska football players and athletes in other sports haven't forgotten Robert C. "Buck" Barger, a trainer who came to their aid after the war. Long-since retired and still suffering the ravages of his D-Day experiences, Buck lives in Wamego, Kansas.

His main duty these days is spreading the Gospel and the glories of the University of Nebraska football team in his area. Friends and benefactors of his training skills in the late 1940s make semi-annual treks to Wamego to visit Buck—footballers Dale Adams, Darwin (Dub) Salestrom, Gail Gade, track ace Ralph King, and trainer-therapist George Sullivan. Sadly, Cletus Fischer, a Husker football star during our school days, has dropped from the crew after a tough battle with cancer.

D-Day left its mark on Buck Barger, but his heroism is legendary. On the early morning of June 6, 1944, he was a paratrooper with the 101st Airborne Division and dropped behind German lines in Normandy. He landed too hard in the hedge rows, suffering a broken leg, fractured pelvis, broken shoulder, and generally shattered body. A medic, he tried to make himself comfortable, but he wasn't found and evacuated for a long time. After months in hospitals, he was scheduled to return home, but he demanded to be sent back to his unit. Caught in heavy action in the Battle of the Bulge, Buck's outfit was overrun by Germans, and he spent the last months of the war in a prisoner of war camp. With typical Buck Barger humor, he told the group, "The Germans didn't bother me when I was lying there all banged up in that field on D-Day, but the damn cows sure bothered the hell out of me."

Rimington Honors

Dave Rimington, Nebraska's center in 1980-81-82, ranks as one of the most decorated college football lineman in the history of the game.

He became the first player to win back-to-back Outland Trophies in 1981-1982, also earning All-

America honors both years and the Lombardi Award in 1982. He has been inducted into the National Football Foundation's College Football Hall of Fame and the Nebraska Football Hall Fame.

Dave was a three-time All-Big Eight center (1980-81-82), and in 1981 was named Big Eight Offensive Player of the Year, the only time the honor has gone to a lineman. He co-captained the 1982 Husker team, and Nebraska retired his No. 50 jersey.

Rimington was also a three-time Academic All-Big Eight honoree and twice was named Academic All-America. He was a National Football Foundation Scholar-Athlete, and in 1982 he was named an NCAA Top Five Student-Athlete.

An Omaha native, Dave was drafted in the first round by Cincinnati and played five years in the NFL with the Bengals, then played with the Philadelphia Eagles for two years before retiring in 1989. He is now president of the Boomer Esiason Foundation, headquartered in New York City.

Rimington's sense of humor matches his football prowess. Once asked by the media if he had a real close relationship with Coach Tom Osborne, he joked, "I'm not sure, the only time he has ever talked to me was when he thought I was going to the NFL draft early."

Rich Glover

Rich Glover became one of Nebraska's most decorated defensive players, but that came after a slow start as a sophomore in 1970. Reason? Defensive tackle Larry Jacobson, a 6-7 junior, who would win the 1971 Outland Trophy.

Rookie Glover backed up "Jake" during Nebraska's run to a first national championship, but he didn't see much action. After the season, Coach Bob Devaney and defensive line coach Monte Kiffin made one of their greatest moves—Glover from tackle to middle guard.

The 6-1 former tackle made every All-Big Eight and All-America that picked a middle guard as a junior and senior. He won three ABC- Chevrolet scholarships for TV performances, won the Outland Trophy as a senior, twice was a finalist for the Lombardi Award and won it in 1972. Rich was twice named the Outstanding Lineman in the Orange Bowl (against Alabama in 1972 and Notre Dame in 1973), and the American Coaches Association named him the Kodak Player of the Year in 1972.

Coach Devaney summed up Glover's career: "Rich Glover was the greatest defensive lineman I've ever seen. We took him for granted some of the time because he never had a bad game. He always played from great to super and forced other teams to do things they wouldn't ordinarily do."

While Glover and Jacobson didn't "team" together in 1970, they were key members of the 1971 unbeaten Nebraska team that won the national title. And both had a dramatic impact on the Oklahoma Sooners in the 1971 "Game of the Century," won by the Cornhuskers, 35-31. Jacobson has had a long career as an investment counselor, and Glover is an assistant coach on Coach Tony Samuel's staff at New Mexico State University.

The Terrific Trio

Colorado-Nebraska football games almost always have had a dose of the unexpected tossed in for the fans. Such was the case in 1983 when the Cornhuskers held a slim 14-12 lead at halftime, then exploded for 48 points in the third quarter to ensure a 69-19 win at Lincoln's Memorial Stadium. Nebraska had a potent offensive unit led by Heisman winner Mike Rozier, All-America wingback Irving Fryar, and All-America quarterback Turner Gill. But even the most exuberant fan or clairvoyant sports writer would not have predicted a 48-point bonanza for the Huskers. That had never occurred in Big Eight Conference history, and it missed the NCAA record by a mere one point.

The Husker "Terrific Trio" produced three touchdowns in the first 2:24 minutes of the third quarter—Fryar ran 54 yards, Rozier next ran 13 yards, and Gill followed with a 17-yard scoring dash. Scott Livingston kicked three points, and it was 35-12.

Rozier had established a Nebraska record with his 32nd touchdown in the first quarter, and he got his second TD of the third quarter (18 yards) for No. 34.

Fryar logged his second TD with a 34-yard pass reception from Gill. Jeff Smith added a 12-yard rushing touchdown, before alternate quarterback Nate Mason hit alternate wingback Shane Swanson with a one-yard TD strike to end the third-quarter onslaught. Livingston had gone 4-5 on PAT kicks, and alternate Dave Schneider chipped in two more.

Rozier wound up with 155 yards on 19 carries before retiring after the third TD of the day and 34th of his Husker career.

That's Why We Practice

Mike Rozier was never easily ruffled during his career. He became Nebraska's most productive I-back (4,780 yards, 7.16 average-per-carry, 49 touchdowns and 26 games of 100 or more yards), and no Husker player probably ever had as much fun playing the game.

Rozier had a huge supply of confidence to go with great football ability, and he was also blessed with a sense of humor.

On one occasion, Coach Tom Osborne was meeting with players and noted a number of areas that needed improvement if the Cornhuskers were to continue performing at a high level. Mike reassured the coach, saying, "Coach, that's why we practice!"

Mike Rozier became Nebraska's top rusher in 1983.

Second Chances

Jeff Kinney came out of McCook, Nebraska, as a highly rated high school athlete and gained Cornhusker immortality in the 1971 "Game of the Century" victory over Oklahoma.

But he had to beg backfield coach Mike Corgan for another chance after fumbling three times against Oklahoma State as a sophomore in 1969. Kinney was so shaken by his performance, he asked to be excused from talking to the press that day and later. However, Corgan—and head coach Bob Devaney—had faith in the 6-2, 210-pound halfback. They gave him many opportunities to play and become a star, and Jeff even resumed talking to reporters.

Injuries hit the I-back position in 1969, and Kinney was installed in the Husker offense's hot spot. He played a key role in helping Nebraska tie for the Big Eight championship. After moving to I-back, Kinney wound up as the conference "Sophomore of the Year", thanks to rushing for the most yards since Bobby Reynolds in 1950 (590), setting a Nebraska reception record with 44 catches and leading the Huskers with 10 touchdowns and 74 points.

Against Oklahoma at Norman, Jeff overshadowed Sooner Heisman winner Steve Owen by carrying 35 times for 127 yards and three TDs in a 44-14 Husker win.

Kinney would sink the Sooners again in his senior season, rushing for 171 yards and four touchdowns—including the winning one in the final moments of the

35-31 win, now known as the "Game of the Century." Jeff split time with Joe Orduna at I-back in 1970 and rushed for 694 yards in Nebraska's successful run for its first national title, and in 1971 he led the Huskers in rushing with 1,037 yards, finished one TD behind Heisman winner Johnny Rodgers (16), caught 23 passes for 253 yards and averaged 18.1 yards on nine kickoff returns in a repeat No. 1 season. He earned All-America and all-conference honors on the football field and also in the classroom.

Kinney later played four years with the NFL Kansas City Chiefs and one year with the then-Buffalo Bills. Way back in 1969, a Nebraska sophomore asked for a second chance, got it, and made the most out of that opportunity—to say the least.

Better Than Coach Devaney?

David Humm now battles against the ravages of MS the same way he fought on the football field—with courage, class, determination, and good humor. As a sophomore, Humm passed to Johnny Rodgers during JR's successful Heisman Trophy race, and the Las Vegas quarterback still reigns as Nebraska's top passer.

Dave holds the top marks for career yards (5,035), season yards (2,074), game yards (297), career (637) and season attempts (266), per-game average (152.6), consecutive game completions (15), touchdowns in consecutive games (10), career completions (353). He also holds five of the Top 10 marks for passing yards in a game and holds three spots in Top 10 season passing yards.

Husker players were well aware of the extreme pressure on Tom Osborne in 1973 when he succeeded Bob Devaney as head coach. Fans and the media constantly compared Osborne to Devaney. During a mid-season Thursday practice at the passing station, players pressed Osborne to show them how a former NFL receiver caught a pass.

Finally, Osborne split out, ran down the field, and leaped to catch a pass from back-up quarterback Steve Runty. Just as the ball reached Osborne, a defensive back slammed into him and knocked him down.

As the deflected ball bounced on the turf, Dave Humm—in a loud voice—said, "Coach Devaney would have held on to that one!"

Following graduation, Humm was drafted by Oakland and played four years for the Raiders as back-up quarterback and kick-holder. He also played one year at Buffalo and one at Baltimore before returning to the Raiders in 1983 and 1984 before launching a career in sports television.

Loosen Up, Junior

Junior Miller ranks as one of Nebraska's best tight ends since the reinstatement of two-platoon football. The 6-4, 222-pounder from Midland, Texas, became the Huskers' tight end career reception yards leader during the 1977-78-79 seasons.

Now the successful owner and CEO of Miller Mailing Co. in Lincoln, Miller ranks as the No. 9 receiver in the Husker record book with 61 career catches for 1,123 yards. He averaged 18.4 yards per catch and scored 13 touchdowns. Twice named All-Big Eight, he earned All-America honors in 1979, when he tied the GNU tight end records with seven touchdown receptions.

Blessed with a deep voice and a hearty laugh, Junior was a favorite among players and coaches for his relaxed personality—until game time.

Pregame meals were normally quiet affairs during Tom Osborne's tenure as head coach—much the same as any other team's routine. Coaches and players began heavy concentration on the task ahead at meal time.

Prior to the 1978 Nebraska-Kansas game in Lawrence, the Cornhuskers were reverently consuming the pregame meal when the silence was shattered by a booming laugh supplied by Junior Miller.

Silence once again quickly returned, and assistant coach John Melton said to Coach Osborne, "Tom, we've got to do something about loosening up Junior—he seems awfully tight this morning!" Nebraska won the game, 63-21.

"Mr. Touchdown USA"

Bobby Reynolds arrived on the Nebraska campus already established as one of the state's most celebrated high school athletes. The Grand Island native had excelled in football, basketball, and baseball, earned a multitude of prep honors. He also became a baseball draftee by the Chicago White Sox.

However, in 1950 when Bobby launched his sophomore season on second-year coach Bill Glassford's squad, there was no hint he would became the glamour boy of college football that fall. What a surprise unfolded, as the young Cornhusker performed brilliantly in leading the nation in scoring 157 points and rushed

Husker Mike Rozier and Bobby Reynolds rally with "Fox."

for 1,342 yards. That mark wasn't broken until Mike Rozier ran for 1,689 yards in 1982.

Injuries dogged Reynolds—separated shoulder, lime in his eyes and a broken leg—during his final two seasons, but memories of his sophomore explosion are legendary. Bobby still ranks No. 13 on the career rushing chart (2,196 yards, 5.81 average and 24 touchdowns) and leads the field in season points per game (17.4 in 1950, with 22 TDs and 25 PATs), points per game, career (9.2 with 211 points in 1950-51-52). He is tied with Ahman Green (1997) with 22 season touchdowns behind Mike Rozier's 29 in 1983. Reynolds sophomore yardage remained a Husker record until Lawrence Phillips piled up 1,722 yards in 1994.

Nebraska fans vividly recall Reynolds' amazing run against Missouri in 1950, when he ran all over the field several times eluding Tigers before finally breaking clear to score in a 40-34 win. Bobby scored all of Nebraska's points in his debut against Indiana, a 20-20 tie, and he never let down.

In the Big Seven showdown at Norman in 1950, the game was billed as a personal battle between Nebraska's Bobby Reynolds and Oklahoma's Billy Vessels, and that it was. Oklahoma won the game, 49-35, behind Vessels, who would win the Heisman as a senior, but Ramblin' Robert scored 21-points in the first half to stay even with the Sooners.

Always a class act, the late Lincoln insurance executive made his way to the Sooner locker room following the 1950 loss to OU. The nation's leading scorer wanted to congratulate Vessels and his victorious team-mates.

It was a fitting end to an unforgettable football season for "Mr. Touchdown, USA." Incidentally, the Cornhusker Marching Band still plays that stirring song in pre-kickoff programs at Memorial Stadium.

Taking a Breather

Johnny Rodgers not only is a Heisman Trophy winner and Nebraska's all-time pass receiver, he has always possessed a sense of humor. Rodgers never missed games because of injury and took some brutal hits after snaring high deliveries. Tough as he was, he occasionally needed a "breather."

Nebraska's retired trainer and physical therapist George Sullivan remembers one game in which Rodgers took a hard hit and remained on the turf. When the trainers rushed onto the field to check on Johnny's condition, they realized there was hope for his recovery.

"Johnny looked up," Sullivan recalled, "and said, 'Hey, George, how are the fans taking this?'"

Jerry Tagge

Jerry Tagge may be best remembered as the Nebraska quarterback who led Nebraska to a pair of national championships on Bob Devaney's 1970 and 1971

Rich Glover, Willie Harper, "Fox," and Johnny Rodgers warm up for the Orange Bowl.

teams. Especially, his "big reach" in the 1971 Orange Bowl game against Louisiana State. It was Tagge's extension of the football from the top of the pile over the goal-line that gave Nebraska the 17-12 victory and a No. 1 ranking.

Tagge is also remembered for skippering the 13-0 national championship Cornhuskers in 1971, particularly for a scrambling third-down pass to a diving Johnny Rodgers that kept the winning drive alive in the dying minutes of the "Game of the Century" game at Oklahoma on Thanksgiving Day.

But the record book shows Jerry Tagge was a consistent producer and leader during his 1969-70-71 career. He still ranks as the No. 2 career passer in Nebraska history (behind Dave Humm), holds the record for career completion percentage, and four total offense records. Jerry completed 59.9 percent of his passes with only 19 interceptions in 581 attempts, piling up 4,704 yards and 32 touchdowns during his career.

Not known as a "running quarterback," like later Husker stars, Tagge could still ramble when the necessity arose. His 85 yards rushing and 234 yards passing against Missouri in 1971 is still a total offense record. He also holds the sixth-best mark in that category with 82 yards rushing and 219 yards passing against Minnesota in 1969. Jerry owns the best marks in season total offense attempts (107 rushes, 239 passes) and career attempts (255 rushes, 581 passes). He gained 314 yards rushing and 2,019 passing in 1971 to post another Husker record that still stands.

Jerry has always paid tribute to his receivers for his impressive aerial numbers. His targets included Heisman winner Johnny Rodgers (No. 1), Jeff Kinney (No. 2), Guy Ingles (No. 4), Jerry List (No. 9) and Frosty Anderson (No. 23), all standouts in Husker receiving history.

Irving Fryar,
Long-Range Bomb Target

Irving Fryar could be termed Nebraska's long-range bomb target among the Cornhuskers' long list of pass receivers. At least he qualified in 1983, his senior season.

Fryar caught eight touchdowns passes from Turner Gill that fall, and his average touchdown reception was 42.3 yards. A 4.43 speedster from Mt. Holly, New Jersey, Irving was helped by two long receptions against Minnesota and hurt by a measly four-yarder against Missouri.

Nebraska shocked Minnesota 84-13 at the Metrodome in 1983, and the Turner Gill-to-Irving Fryar combination supplied the electricity in the first quarter. Gill hit Fryar with a 68-yard scoring pass to get things rolling, and five minutes later the duo struck again. The Huskers came to the line of scrimmage, Gill looked left and saw no Gophers anywhere near Fryar, split left, flipped the ball to Irving, and watched him glide 70 yards down the sideline to score.

Fryar added a 41-yard touchdown run with two minutes gone in the third quarter and headed for the bench. During the rest of the season, Irving caught touchdown passes of 49 yards against Wyoming, 62 against Oklahoma State, 38 and four against Missouri, 34 against Colorado, and 20 against Iowa State. He also had a 54-yard touchdown run against Colorado.

Irving wound up with 40 catches for 780 yards and a 19.5 average. He finished his Husker career with a rushing average of 11.8 and five touchdowns, a pass reception average of 17.9 and 11 touchdowns and a kickoff return average of 23.8.

Fryar was the first pick in the 1984 draft, going to the New England Patriots, where he stayed for nine years. He then moved on to Miami for three years, Philadelphia for three years, and Washington in 1999 and 2000.

An ordained minister, Irving became a fixture in the game of football.

Ironically, Fryar's teammate Mike Rozier was chosen No.1 pick in the 1983 USFL draft by the Jersey Jets after both had played in the Shrine East-West game and the Japan Bowl. Also worth noting, Irving became the second consensus All-America receiver selected off the nation's No. 1 rushing team. Freeman White of Nebraska was the first to receive that distinction in 1965.

No Sweat

Tommie Frazier made a lot of opponents sweat during his four-year career at quarterback for the Nebraska Cornhuskers. But not nearly as much as he did at his first news media conference.

Frazier got his first Husker start as a freshman at Missouri in 1992, and the Cornhuskers came through with a 34-24 victory. While Tommie never seemed anything other than cool in the great remaining games he directed, he was in a stew the following Tuesday when he faced the news media at the weekly briefing.

"I've never seen anyone sweat as much as Tommie did that day. He looked terrified, and when the TV lights came on, it just poured off him. But he got through it and got better every time he met the media after that," Nebraska SID Chris Anderson recalls.

Tommie wound up his career as Nebraska's most decorated quarterback, despite battling a blood-clot problem that kept him out of eight games during his junior season. But he bounced back from that setback and won Orange Bowl MVP honors, leading Nebraska to its first national championship under Tom Osborne. He directed two fourth-quarter touchdown drives to defeat Miami, 24-17. With Brook Berringer and Matt Turman holding the fort while Frazier was sidelined, the Huskers put together a 13-0 season, and a two-year mark of 24-1-0.

Frazier and the Cornhuskers added another un-beaten season in 1995, going 11-0 and obliterating Florida in the Tostitos Fiesta Bowl, 62-24. That clinched another No. 1 finish and a fourth straight conference title.

The Huskers posted a 36-1-0 record in the 1993-94-95 run, and the highlight for Frazier was a 75-yard touchdown run during which he broke seven tackles. He wound up with 199 yards and another MVP bowl award in the Fiesta romp.

Tommie earned consensus All-America honors and was the 1995 Heisman Trophy runner-up. He left Nebraska with a 32-3 record as a starter and took with him the Johnny Unitas Golden Arm Award and five Nebraska records, including total offense yards (5,476) and touchdowns (79).

The young freshman from Palmetto, Florida, worked up a huge sweat during his first meeting with the media, but he wound up a superstar who graduated with a Communication Studies degree, provided sideline reports for the Pinnacle Nebraska football network, and worked as a public relations staff member for Gov. (now U.S. Senator) Ben Nelson. Frazier now serves as the running back coach for Coach Kevin Steele's Baylor Bears.

Benched

Vince Ferragamo went to three bowl games with the Nebraska Cornhuskers and a Super Bowl with the Los Angeles Rams, but that amounted to one too many bowl games for the handsome transfer from the University of California.

Ferragamo played for the Golden Bears before transferring to Nebraska. He sat out the 1974 season, being groomed as the heir apparent to senior quarterback David Humm. Vince practiced with the Huskers throughout 1974, and Coach Tom Osborne was counting on him for the next two years.

When Nebraska landed a bid to the 1974 Sugar Bowl, the Huskers took the entire squad to New Orleans to play the Florida Gators. Vince was included on the squad because he was the scout team quarterback. That turned out to be a big mistake. In the locker room before the game, Nebraska coaches and the faculty representatives wondered if Ferragamo could suit up and sit on the bench. After much discussion, it was the unanimous feeling that since he had practiced all season, he could suit up, even though he could not play in the game.

Ferragamo was sitting on the Husker bench and was spotted by ABC sideline reporter Jim Lampley, who recognized Vince from his Cal days and did a report on camera. A number of people notified the NCAA that Nebraska had taken an ineligible player to the Sugar Bowl, and they were right. Nebraska learned that if a student-athlete is not eligible to play in the game, he cannot take the trip with the team. Nebraska won the game, 13-10, with Ferragamo on the bench, but Vince had to sit out the 1975 opener because of the illegal bowl trip.

Vince did take the Huskers to the 1975 Fiesta Bowl against Arizona State. But when Nebraska lost 17-14 to Frank Kush's kid—Dan kicked three field goals, the last with 4:50 left in the game to win—Ferragamo may have felt bowl games were not for him. After his first pass early in the game, he was benched, and alternate Terry Luck went the distance while Vince watched from the sideline.

However, Ferragamo did enjoy his final bowl trip with the Cornhuskers. In the 1976 Astro-Bluebonnet Bowl in Houston, Vince hit 14 of 24 passes for 232 yards and two touchdowns. The last TD came on a 23-yard pass to Big Eight 400-meter champ Chuck Malito, producing a 27-24 victory.

While his time at Nebraska was short, Vince still ranks No. 5 on the career passing chart, and his 147.7 NCAA power rating is the best on the Top 10 list. He holds records for most yards in a game (264 vs. Miami in 1976), most season completions (145 in 1976), most season touchdown passes (20), and he ranks No. 2 on season yards passing with 2,071, just three yards behind Dave Humm, his predecessor.

Vince earned All-America and All-Conference football honors, as well as Academic All-America laurels in 1976. After playing in the Hula and Japan Bowls, he was drafted by the NFL Rams and played eight seasons before at Montreal (Canadian Football League), Buffalo, and Green Bay. He was inducted into the Nebraska Football Hall of Fame in 1984.

"Our House"

Sometimes fans take football games too seriously. At least, some did after the 1987 Nebraska-Oklahoma game in Lincoln.

Broderick Thomas was an outstanding outside linebacker for Nebraska, lettering four years from 1985 to 1988 and earning All-Big Eight honors three years, and All-America recognition in 1987 and 1988.

Thomas is one of the most colorful players in Nebraska history. The media loved him for his candor, and the fans loved him for his flamboyant play on the gridiron. Broderick loved to win, and frustration set in when Oklahoma beat the Huskers 27-7 in 1985 and 20-17 at Lincoln in a 1986 heartbreaker. Thomas vowed it would never happen again. The Big Eight schedule had the Sooners returning to Lincoln again in 1987, and Broderick many times said, "They can't beat us in our house two years in a row!"

As the game approached, "Our House" became the battle cry of the fans, the team, and especially Broderick. Some enterprising fan produced sets of huge plastic keys on a big ring, a tribute to Broderick's "Our House" campaign. Barry Switzer's Sooners were not intimidated by Broderick's "House," however, and Oklahoma won again, 17-7. After the game, Memorial Stadium clean-up crews found a number of plastic "Our House" keys tossed in urinals located in the men's rooms. Deposited, no doubt, by disheartened Husker fans.

A member of the Nebraska Football Hall of Fame, Thomas was a first-round choice of Tampa Bay in the 1989 NFL draft and played five years with the Bucs, then finished a 10-year career with the Detroit Lions in 1994, the Minnesota Vikings in 1995, and three years with the Dallas Cowboys.

5

Going Bowling

Not a Place to Visit

Coach Bob Devaney always wanted to win bowl games, like any other football game the Huskers played, but he also felt strongly that a bowl game was a reward for a successful season, and players should have some fun.

When the Huskers went to the Sun Bowl in 1969, a small group of players had a little too much fun on a night trip to Juarez, across the Rio Grande from El Paso. They wound up in the Juarez jail, never a nice spot to visit, and Sun Bowl officials and Devaney rushed across the border to bail out the players.

Devaney confronted the group in jail and proceeded to give them a hellfire-and-brimstone lecture about the need for moderation and good citizenship.

But he was speechless when one of the players interrupted his chewing session and said, "Well, at least, Coach, we go to church on Sunday!"

Bob answered by giving the player a swift kick in the butt, then arranged to spring the wayward players.

Disturbing the Peace?

Coach Tom Osborne had to take a trip to jail in New Orleans, and I had to take a trip to court prior to the 1987 Sugar Bowl.

Hard as it was to believe, then as is now, a small group of players was arrested one night as they were walking back to the team hotel for curfew. Reason?— disturbing the peace on Bourbon Street! Sugar Bowl officials and Osborne retrieved the players from jail and a check of events indicated a miscarriage of justice. It seemed the players were heading home and their wives were singing, "We're Off to See The Wizard," in honor of Coach Osborne, when a patrol car pulled up, and the officer, who may have been an LSU fan, made a wisecrack, which was ignored by the Husker group. The officer circled the block, stopped the car and called the paddy wagon when the players questioned the reason for being stopped. As the players were herded into the van for the ride to jail, they asked, "What about our wives?" and were told by the officers, "Let them walk to the hotel."

Sugar Bowl officials were upset and so were Osborne, athletic director Bob Devaney, and the entire Nebraska party. City officials, likewise, felt the incident should not have happened. However, the mayor and the chief of police were also in a position of supporting an officer, while realizing that the Nebraska players had done little to upset the noise level on Bourbon Street at 10:45 at night.

So a meeting of all parties involved was held the next morning. On hand in the Sugar Bowl suite in the team hotel were Nebraska athletic department and university administrators, the Sugar Bowl president and other bowl committeemen, the chief of police, prosecuting attorney and the judge who would try the case. After a lengthy discussion, the University of Nebraska and the City of New Orleans reached a settlement:

If the players would sign a statement releasing the city from any legal action for false arrest and imprisonment, the judge would rule a miscarriage of justice, and the records of the players would be expunged.

I was given the documents and was asked to contact the players for their signatures.

On the day of the court hearing, I delivered the signed documents to the judge in his chambers, enjoying a cup of coffee with him until court opened. When the players' case was called, the charges were read, and the judge ruled the charges were improper, akin to unwarranted arrest, and cleared the records of all concerned. He concluded the case by adding, "If there any questions about this case, the press can meet me in my chambers."

No one showed up while we had another cup of coffee. Case closed, and Nebraska beat LSU in the Superdome, 30-15.

Pleasant Practice

Bowl trips always involve social gatherings with university staffs and host committee people. Bob Devaney wanted to get his bowl teams some warm weather practice time, and he took teams to Brownsville, Texas, twice (1964 and 1966) and to Scottsdale, Arizona's Camelback Inn in 1965. Shortly thereafter, the NCAA passed legislation requiring schools wishing to train off campus to do so only within 100 miles of the game site.

Border Buttermilk Festivities

Brownsville hospitality, like that of the Sun Bowl, was warm, friendly, and full of Texas conviviality. One night in Brownsville, the hospitality committee roasted a cow's head at a "Border Buttermilk" party for the Devaney coaching staff after practice.

Border Buttermilk, we learned, is a refreshing batch of blended Margaritas. While the group sipped the icy Buttermilk, the hosts unwrapped a cow's head that had been wrapped in some sort of paper and buried in a pit full of hot coals. We were all invited to grab a tortilla and tear off some roasted meat from the skull and enjoy the good life. It was a delicious treat, once you realized the cow was out of its misery. Devaney's backfield coach was Mike Corgan, a former Michigan high school coach like Bob, who had played at Notre Dame before World War II navy service.

Dining was a challenge for Mike, and he was at his best around the cow's head. But, as the tender meat was stripped from the skull, Mike got down to serious eating by grabbing the skull, ripping open the jaw and pulling out the tongue. He carved slices of tongue meat for his tortilla's and was never happier as his fellow coaches and Brownsville friends cheered his courage.

But a host decided to put Corgan to the ultimate test. Unnoticed by anyone, he prepared a special tortilla and handed it to Mike. "Try this delicacy," he said. Mike eagerly took the tortilla and opened it to see what he was about to consume. It was one of the cow's eyeballs, staring up at Mike, and his appetite ran up the white flag. "I'm not eating that damned thing," he roared amidst cries of "Chicken!" from Devaney and the gang.

Corgan vs. Lobster

Mike Corgan's reputation as a tough, demanding backfield coach was well deserved, based on his playing days at Notre Dame, his success as a high school coach in Michigan, and a Bob Devaney assistant at Wyoming before coming to Nebraska.

But he never lived down the fact that a lobster whipped him at an Orange Bowl party. The grand affair was held at a hotel on Biscayne Boulevard and featured cocktails, dining, and dancing. One of the top food attractions was a long table covered by lobster tails. Mike, like everyone else, enjoyed the seafood delicacy, but he had his eye on the table's centerpiece—a huge, bright orange lobster, surely the king of the deep with giant claws. After several dares from Coach Devaney and assistant Jim Ross, Mike charged the table and scooped up the centerpiece and returned to his table.

Entertainment for spectators and frustration for Mike commenced at once.

Despite furious attempts to smash the claws, the lobster fought back. In desperation, Mike removed a shoe and began pounding the claws while onlookers cheered encouragement. Lobster 2, Coach Corgan 0.

A competitor to the end, Mike then put King Lobster on the floor, climbed up on his chair and jumped down on his adversary. His aim was good, but little edible lobster meat survived his final assault. Devaney and Ross scored the match as a clear victory for the lobster, but did award Mike high marks for degree of difficulty and persistence.

That's a Lotta Bowls

Bowl games are a lot of work for coaches, support staff people, and the players. Old Fox has 34 Nebraska bowl game battle stars, dating back to 1954. Bill Glassford's Huskers wound up in the 1955 Orange Bowl against Duke, because the Big Seven rules prevented champion Oklahoma from repeating the trip. My second Husker bowl assignment came in 1962 when Bob Devaney's first team went 8-2 and gained a bid to the Gotham Bowl in New York. I wound up 1-1 working as a sportswriter. Duke won the Orange Bowl, 34-7, while Nebraska edged Miami, 36-34, in the frigid Yankee Stadium game.

Little did I know when I became the Husker SID in 1963 that Devaney and Tom Osborne would get me to 32 bowl games during the next 34 years. The *CoSIDA Digest*, house organ for the College Sports Information Directors of America organization, lists me as the SID leader with 28 bowl trips and 24 bowls in succession.

The 34 Nebraska bowl trips include 16 Oranges, five Fiestas, four Sugars, three Cottons, two Suns, single jaunts to the Liberty, Astro-Bluebonnet, Florida Citrus, and the Gotham Bowl.

Looking back, I enjoyed every one of the bowl games I attended, thanks to the friendliness and hospitality of the host committees. However, I confess to almost freezing at the Gotham Bowl, but dinner at Mama Leone's and a victory party with the Devaney staff at the Upstairs at the Downstairs eased the pain of frostbite.

The Gotham Bowl

Any memory of the Gotham Bowl includes 1) very few fans because a newspaper strike in New York kept the game a secret; 2) the ice-covered turf and 14-degree temperature; 3) Miami's George Mira passing for 321 yards and losing, 36-34; and 4) Nebraska almost not making the trip to New York.

Nebraska was guaranteed $35,000 to play in the game, but NU Chancellor Clifford Hardin stipulated cash-on-the-barrel head: the money had to be in hand, or the team couldn't fly out of Lincoln. While the team gathered in the airport, a Nebraska group was in New York—ticket manager Jim Pittenger, SID John Bentley, Regent Clarence Swanson (a Hall of Fame end in the 1920s), Dick Becker, and Fox covering for the Lincoln newspapers.

Gotham Bowl promoter Robert Curran delivered a check for $35,000, but a bank would not certify it when "Pitt" and Bentley went for verification. They called the airport to report the news, and the flight continued to be delayed while the promoter arranged to assure certification of the Husker guarantee.

Curran was successful, and a call to the Lincoln airport got the green light for take-off. It took some doing, but the stage was set for one of the greatest college football games that very few people were able to see. Nebraska countered Mira with Thunder Thornton's running, Willie Ross' 92-yard kickoff return and a last-minute interception of Mira's desperation pass by Bob Brown to clinch the win.

Unforgettable, also, are Bob Devaney's final pre-game comments to his squad while the players were donning tennis shoes because of icy field conditions in the Gotham Bowl. Bob gathered the team and said, "I really feel bad about getting you guys into this mess today. I know it's a terrible day and this won't be much fun, but it kind of reminds me of the old back-alley fights we used to have when I was a kid in Michigan. There's nobody here to watch, but the toughest son-of-a-bitch is going to win!"

Cheers erupted as the Huskers skated out to a near-empty Yankee Stadium and delivered Devaney the first of his six bowl victories, 36-34. Devaney retired after winning a third straight Orange Bowl game, 40-6, over Notre Dame. He was 6-3 in postseason play, winning four Orange Bowls (Auburn, LSU, Alabama, Notre Dame) and losing at the Cotton (Arkansas), Orange (Alabama) and Sugar (Alabama).

Watch Out for Rats

Nebraska's long-time head trainer and physical therapist George Sullivan will never forget his last trip to the Sun Bowl in 1980. Sun Bowl hospitality committeemen took Tom Osborne and the staff to Juarez for dinner and entertainment. As we were walking into the restaurant, one of the hosts said, "This place is really fun. It has great food and entertainment. Once in a while, though, they get a rat in there, but not very often."

Nobody thought anything about it, and we gathered around a large table for cocktails before dinner. A comedian joined us and told a couple of jokes and everyone was talking when someone hollered, "It's a damn rat !" as George let out a yell and jumped out of his chair.

The bowl guys shook their heads and cussed the rat, but indicated it wouldn't happen again. A few minutes later, someone else hollered "Rats" and Sullivan yelled and climbed up on his chair.

It was then we learned that a small Mexican boy was hidden under the table and when someone yelled "It's a rat!" he brushed a broom straw across George's ankle. When the players learned of George's battle with the "rat," they presented him with a toy mouse during a training room ceremony.

Strong Words

Husker coach Tom Osborne almost always had his teams in high spirits, but his approach was less bombastic than Devaney's. Tom relied on thorough preparation, great conditioning, and only an occasional "Dadgummit" to arouse the Huskers to fever pitch.

Nebraska coach Tom Osborne

However, in the 1974 Sugar Bowl, Tom abandoned "Dad- gummit" in favor of a more definitive pep talk. At halftime of the game with Florida, Nebraska was trailing, 10-0. The Huskers held the usual routine with position coaches until it was time to go back on the field.

At that point, Osborne started talking loudly and sternly to his players about what was needed in the second half. He concluded by yelling, "You guys know what you're going to do in the second half? I'll tell you what you're going to do—you're going to kick the hell out of Florida!"

Split end Skeeter Malito, who had been sitting on a pop cooler, jumped up and said, "Jesus Christ, he's never said that before!"

Perhaps Tom's halftime assurance that the Huskers would play better in the second half paid dividends. Nebraska's defensive Black Shirts shut out the Gators, while fullback Tony Davis led a resurgent offense to a 13-10 victory. Davis rushed for 126 yards, sophomore I-back Monte Anthony scored a touchdown with 13:24 left in the game, and Mike Coyle kicked two field goals to provide the sixth-straight Husker goal victory.

Oh, yes, I had never heard Coach Osborne utter a cuss word before that Sugar Bowl game, and I haven't heard anything but "Dad-gummit" since.

Pep Talks

Bob Liggett was a big, strong defensive tackle on Nebraska's 1969 team that tied for the Big Eight title and met Georgia in the Sun Bowl in El Paso, Texas.

Nebraska wound up winning the game, 40-6, but the outcome may have been influenced at a joint team party a couple of days before. The Huskers and the Bulldogs gathered for a banquet, and during the program, both coaches were introduced. Georgia's Vince Dooley, one of the great coaches and an outstanding athletic director, received polite applause and gave a short talk.

Bob Devaney was introduced, and the NU team, staff, and wives jumped to their feet and gave the Husker coach a long ovation. He, too, gave a short talk, and then a player from each team was asked to say a few words.

Liggett went to the microphone when his turn came, turned to the Georgia players and said, "I'd like to wish all you Georgia boys a lot of luck—but you all know where it's at!"

Nebraska players roared and gave Liggett a standing ovation. Devaney's pregame warning sent the Huskers on the field with enthusiasm. He said, "Let's go out there and do a good job—but be careful running on the field, because half the state of Nebraska is out there in a spirit line waiting for you, and the other half is back home praying for you."

Paul Rogers kicked four field goals, and Jeff Kinney ran 11 yards for a touchdown to give the Huskers an

18-0 lead in the first quarter, sending Nebraska on its way to a national title in 1970.

Race Relations

The 1964 Orange Bowl game had a number of related side issues that would never happen in college football today.

Coach Bob Devaney wanted the team to stay at the Ivanhoe Hotel in Bal Harbor because it was relatively isolated, and the Husker team would fill most of the rooms. Also, the team could practice in a field adjacent to the hotel, and there would be no need to travel away from the beach.

It wasn't easy to arrange. The Ivanhoe was reluctant to house African-American members of the Nebraska team. However, Bob prevailed on that issue by agreeing to the hotel's request that those members not swim in the pool with the other guests. That agreement didn't last long, because the whole team jumped into the pool one afternoon, and no guests fainted.

Practice was difficult because the adjacent field was nothing but sand and weeds. It only took a couple of sessions before bus rides to better facilities were launched. One problem that worried Devaney and his staff was the fact that Auburn had never played against a team that had African-Americans before, and they feared Nebraska players might face problems.

Bob Brown, Bob Devaney's first All-American.

On the morning of the game, Bob asked me to talk to Bob Brown, the All-America guard and linebacker who was 6-5 and weighed 300. I visited with Brown and urged him not to be intimidated, and he laughed, looked down at me, and said, "Relax, Mr. Bryant, I've long had a deep-seeded animosity toward the great state of Alabama." End of worry.

His huge block, which could drive a Tiger player about 30 yards, paved the way for Dennis Claridge's 68-yard touchdown run on the second play of the game. Bob starred for 10 years in the NFL and entered the College Football Hall of Fame in 1993.

"Cut the Line"

Willie Ross was a fine halfback on Bob Devaney's 1963 squad, and he also knew the value of a dollar.

Always a highlight on any of the Orange Bowl visits to Miami was a deep-sea outing arranged by the Orange Bowl Committee. It was great fun for players, most of whom had never seen the ocean before.

Several times competition was arranged between the two schools, with trophies awarded to the winners. Willie was on the deep-sea expedi-

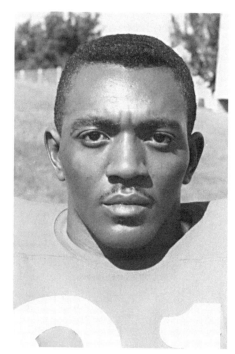

Willie Ross

tion in 1963 and hit the jackpot of fishing. He hooked a very large, beautiful sailfish, truly a magnificent trophy fish, and brought it to the boat.

Observers urged Willie to have the prize catch mounted and he thought it was a great idea for a minute or two. That is, until he asked how much it would cost him, and the skipper said, "I'd say at least $500 or maybe more."

Willie looked lovingly at his beautiful fish and said, "Uhhh, cut the line!"

"We're No. 1!"

College football games can cause pressure to build within players, coaches, and fans.

When Nebraska played LSU in the 1971 Orange Bowl, the Huskers did not anticipate winning the national championship before New Year's Day. After all, Texas was No. 1 and Ohio State was No. 2, leaving No. 3 Nebraska with only hope that both the Longhorns and the Buckeyes would lose.

But when Notre Dame upset Texas in the Cotton Bowl, 24-11, Nebraska players began to get excited. Then the Rose Bowl started, and Stanford was giving Ohio State a tough time as the Huskers boarded buses for the Orange Bowl. Tensions grew as the ride moved slowly away from Miami Beach, and then a huge traffic jam stopped the buses, still a long way from the Bowl.

Minutes dragged on, and the buses couldn't move. The silence was suddenly shattered as Husker middle guard Ed Periard jumped out into the aisle and yelled, "Get this damn bus rolling!" During warm-ups, the word was flashed to the Orange Bowl that Stanford had beaten Ohio State, 27-17, and Nebraska players celebrated in the locker room before the kickoff. Coach Devaney tried to calm them and warned of a tough game ahead, but the Huskers kept yelling, "No sweat, coach. We'll win it. We're No. 1!" Both the coach and the team were right. It was a tough game, Nebraska did win, 17-12, and Nebraska was No. 1.

6

Planes, Trains &
Automobiles

Train Travel

In the 1950s, the media still traveled by train most of the time. On trips to Pittsburgh, for example, we found a way to double our value to our papers.

Dick Becker of *The Lincoln Journal,* Wally Provost of The *Omaha World Herald,* and I would leave Pittsburgh on the train Saturday night and arrive in Chicago Sunday morning.

We would get a hotel room in the Loop, write our Monday copy, take it to Western Union for dispatch and head for Soldier Field to watch the Chicago Bears battle an NFL opponent. After three quarters, we'd grab a cab to Union Station and board the train for Nebraska.

It wasn't all bad. We could pick up column material at the Bears' game, have dinner in the diner, arrive home about midnight—and avoid those dreaded airplane rides.

"Fix it Yourself"

Dick Becker had a bizarre flight from Pittsburgh after one Nebraska-Pitt game. We were aboard a TWA Super Constellation headed for Chicago, and Dick spotted what looked like oil flowing on the wing. He pondered the situation and finally asked the stewardess about it. In a few minutes, a salty pilot with a 50-mission cap walked down the aisle and when he got by Dick, he looked out the window and yelled, "Oh, my God!"

Startled, Dick asked, "What's the matter?" And the pilot said, "Sir, we are losing oil. Our calculations indicate we are losing one pint of oil every 72 years." Passengers giggled, and Dick blushed, "OK, but there's some noise or grinding sound underneath my seat." The pilot got on his knees in the aisle and pounded the floor, yelling, "Knock it off down there!" then headed for the cockpit.

A couple of minutes later, the pilot returned to our seat row carrying a hammer, screw driver and other tools. He dumped them by Becker and said, "Sir, if you don't like the way my airplane runs, you get down there and fix it yourself!" TWA's answer to Steve Canyon returned to the cockpit and managed to find Chicago. But poor Becker's ordeal wasn't over.

As we taxied to the ramp, the stewardess stopped by Dick and said, "Are you all right now, sir, or should I ask the pilot to radio ahead for a wheelchair for you?"

Becker swore he was going to sue the airline, but he didn't. Instead, he left the newspaper to become general manager of Omaha's Ak-Sar-Ben race track. Old Bucket Hips always did prefer horses to airplanes.

Gade, the First Husker Flyer

In 1946, Coach Bernie Masterson's team trained to Oklahoma and lost to the Sooners, 27-6, in Norman. After the game, the squad and entourage again boarded the train and headed for Los Angeles to play UCLA the following Saturday.

As a footnote in history, Husker reserve fullback Gail Gade became the first Nebraska player to fly to a football game. A Nebraska player was injured in the Oklahoma game, and Coach Masterson called Lincoln and ordered Gade to fly to Los Angeles and meet the team when the train pulled in.

Gade's presence wasn't enough to stop the Bruins. UCLA ended the Cornhusker season by winning, 18-0, and the Nebraska team chugged back to Lincoln after almost two weeks in Pullman cars.

Gade launched a career with the Lincoln Police Department after graduation and later served with distinction for many years as the University of Nebraska's campus police chief.

Long Rides

Nebraska's 1940 team traveled to Pasadena for the Rose Bowl game with Stanford, and thousands of Cornhusker fans and students marched to the Burlington Depot to send the players and coaches off with a huge rally.

Like trips to Pittsburgh, the Rose Bowl squad's train did not speed directly to Pasadena. Coach Biff Jones arranged to break up the long trip by stopping in Scottsdale, Arizona. The Huskers stayed at the famed Camelback Inn and logged warm-weather practice time before continuing on to Sunny California.

Twenty-five years later, Bob Devaney took his Orange Bowl-bound team to the Camelback Inn for warm-weather preparation for Bear Bryant's Crimson Tide. After unseasonably cool weather and a near-Monsoon rain, the Huskers flew to Miami.

Neither training session at Camelback Inn paid victory dividends for Nebraska. Stanford beat Nebraska, 21-13, in the Rose Bowl, and Alabama beat the Huskers, 39-28, in the Orange Bowl to win the AP national championship.

Snake Watch

Tom Ash of the *Omaha World Herald* and I were in Baton Rouge early for the Nebraska-Louisiana State game in the 1975 season opener, and LSU's legendary SID Paul Manasseh arranged for a Tiger booster to take us on a bass fishing trip in the Achafalaya Swamp.

Our excursion started in the darkness at 5 a.m., and we rode for an hour or more down narrow channels and across lake-size areas of water. It was foggy, and in the narrow stream areas our guide was always looking up at the moss-covered trees that hung over our heads. I finally asked him why he was looking up at the trees and he said, "Looking for snakes. We don't want one dropping in the boat."

That dulled my interest in finding a good spot for bass fishing, but we continued on and finally started fishing. Neither Tom nor I had any idea where we were or how to get back to civilization, and we never did have any luck finding bass. But we did see a lot of beautiful scenery and had a few exciting moments.

As we were trolling down one narrow stream, our guide whispered, "Be real quiet, here comes a big water moccasin and we don't want him to come in the boat."

I whispered, "What do we do if it comes in the boat?

Tiger Guide whispered back, "We get the hell out!"

Charlie McClendon's Tigers tied the No. 7-ranked Cornhuskers, 6-6, and I've always considered him one of my favorite coaching friends. He retired from coaching and did a great job for the American Football Coaches Association, serving as executive director.

Nebraska had remarkable good luck against LSU in a six-game series. The Huskers won a thrilling 17-12 come-from-behind game in the 1971 Orange Bowl to win their first national title. NU won the 1975 home opener, 10-7, followed by a 21-20 squeaker in the 1983 Orange Bowl; the 6-6 tie at Baton Rouge; a 28-10 win in the 1985 Orange Bowl and a 30-15 victory in the 1987 Orange Bowl.

Strong Medicine

The United States Military Academy at West Point is a beautiful place to visit in the fall. Historic fortifications and buildings are framed by trees shining with brilliant colors in the sunshine.

In 1957, Bill Jennings' first year as Nebraska's head football coach, the Cornhuskers played the Cadets at Miche Stadium and lost 42-0, thanks to an impressive display of running by All-American Bob Anderson.

Sportswriters were seated in an open-air press box behind a large number of high-ranking Army officers on the front row. One of America's great sportswriters and a good friend, Sec Taylor of the *Des Moines Register,* was covering the game and had a difficult time. He was nearing the end of his long career and had a hearing problem. A bigger problem bothered all of us—Army scored a lot, made a lot of big plays, and the brass in front of us stood up and cheered a lot.

Sec couldn't hear and he couldn't see much.

Becker and I kept him filled in on the action, so he could file an accurate story for the *Register's* "Peach." Long after the game, with our stories pecked out in the chill of the evening, Taylor, Becker and I left the press box. As we walked slowly through the darkness, Spec stopped and said, "Boy, that was a tough day, I've got to take my heart medicine."

Becker and I both feared our aging friend might be having a heart attack—until he asked, "How are your hearts?" and handed us his small flask, partially filled with excellent bourbon.

Corps on Parade

That 1957 trip to cover the Nebraska-Army football game was memorable for other reasons. Dick Becker and I went to the Military Academy early Saturday morning to see the parade of Cadets. We climbed into a grandstand area and sat down to await the colorful drama, and soon the seats were filled. With the sound of the drums and the Long Gray Line in the distance, two military policemen arrived and asked us to leave.

Unintentionally, we had taken seats in the military brass's reviewing stand, and Becker learned we were seated next to several famous generals. Two former enlisted men apparently were not scheduled to receive a salute from the Cadet Corps that morning, so Becker and I were escorted to the left-field bleachers. But it was a great thrill to watch the Corps on parade.

Skywriters 1, Grim Reaper 0

No sportswriters ever worked harder or had more fun than the Big Eight Skywriters during the Wayne Duke-John Waldorf era. Wayne was the conference commissioner before moving on to the Big 10, and Waldorf was the supervisor of officials.

John was the brother of Lynn "Pappy" Waldorf and officiated college football for many years before joining the Big Eight staff. His assignment during the Skywriters Tour—which moved the media around the league by bus or plane—was to baby-sit the sportswriters and sportscasters. Not an easy chore, by any measure.

Nerves were put to the test when the conference chartered a plane that most resembled an old Ford Trimotor, and the Skywriters were forced to endure a horrible flight into Boulder. When the pilot finally landed the plane, the passengers heard veteran writer Charlie Smith exclaim, as only Charlie could, "Final score—Skywriters 1, Grim damn Reaper 0!"

Near Miss

As baffling as the third-quarter Husker collapse against Michigan was, it certainly didn't match the near tragedy that occurred on the plane trip home from the 1986 Fiesta Bowl game. In fact, the landing in Lincoln was the best "touch down" of the season for all on board—coaches, players, staff members, and family members seated in the huge L-1011.

Shortly after takeoff in Phoenix, a jarring rumble shook the entire airplane and was followed by a smoky smell in the rear. Veteran flyers knew something had gone wrong, but we stayed airborne and continued to have hope. My wife noticed the flight crew no longer seemed friendly and appeared to be uptight. They had good reason for the latter.

The flight continued on to Lincoln, with no word of any trouble. But finally the captain clicked on his radio and said, "We are 40 miles from Lincoln. I don't want to alarm you, but we have lost an engine. We will be landing in a few minutes, and it should be a routine landing. We have two engines, so we expect a normal landing."

There was no panic, but neither was there a festive atmosphere on board. Some no doubt did some praying, some couples held hands, and most held their breath as the giant plane headed down a runway that was lined with crash trucks, fire trucks, and ambulances, all with flashing red lights.

As the plane pulled to the ramp, the captain came back on the intercom and said, "Welcome to Lincoln!" (words that brought loud cheers) and added, "I'm sorry to have alarmed you, but I felt you had a right to know what our situation was."

Knowing he meant "pray," everyone said, "Amen!"

7
Strike Up the Band

A Mean Trumpet

Friday nights during football season used to include some occasional revelry in the post-WWII era. Press parties were the order of the day, or media and school officials got together for libation and cuisine on road trips if press parties were not scheduled.

Prior to the 1954 Nebraska-Sooner game, Dick Becker of *The Lincoln Journal* and I joined Nebraska athletic director Bill Orwig and ticket manager A.J. (Lew) Lewandowski for a nightcap in the Leopard Lounge of the Skirvin Hotel in Oklahoma City.

Orwig, relatively new as the Husker AD, became somewhat irritated, because the house band kept playing "Boomer Sooner" every 15 minutes or so. He kept asking the bandleader to play "There is No Place Like Nebraska," to no avail, because the leader explained they didn't know the song and had no music.

Dick Becker, Bobby Reynolds, and Don Bryant.

Becker happened to mention that "Fox plays the trumpet, and he knows how to play 'No Place.' " That sent Lewandowski to the bandstand, and after a conference with the bandleader, the crowd heard the announcement: "We're lucky to have with us the Chancellor of the University of Nebraska who will join us to play "There Is No Place Like Nebraska . . . Ladies and gentlemen, Chancellor Clifford Hardin!"

Lewandowski pushed me to the bandstand while the crowd cheered, and a trumpet player handed me his horn. I hit "No Place" on the borrowed trumpet and the second time around the band joined in. Bill

Orwig was elated, but I hope Chancellor Hardin never heard about the night he played the trumpet in Oklahoma City.

Swing and Sway
with Sammy Kay

The University of Nebraska has a long and colorful history of outstanding music during football games at Memorial Stadium, and the Cornhusker Marching Band, blaring "There Is No Place Like Nebraska," brings Husker fans leaping to their feet.

Prior to World War II, the band that performed at football games represented the Army ROTC unit on campus. It wasn't until the late 1930s that Prof. Don Lentz managed to have the band shed the olive drab Army uniforms in favor of Scarlet and Cream outfits. Aging Nebraska fans still get chills remembering the Cornhusker Marching Band strutting smartly in their new uniforms during the Rose Bowl parade on New Year's Day, 1941.

Legend has it that the Nebraska band was the first to march and play throughout the entire parade route in Pasadena. At least, the Husker band holds the conference record for Rose Bowl appearances, since no other conference school has played in a Rose Bowl.

In the early years, of the 20th century, the Nebraska band gained recognition and fan following under the baton of director Billy Quick. Enthusiasm for band entertainment at football games continued to grow as the football program progressed.

On the eve of World War II, famed band leader Sammy Kaye ("Swing and Sway With Sammy Kaye") brought his band to Lincoln to play a gig at the University of Nebraska's Military Ball, following a football game. Prof. Lentz invited Sammy to attend the game and take part in the halftime show.

It was a memorable afternoon at Memorial Stadium when Sammy Kaye directed the Cornhusker Marching Band in the popular swing tune of that era, "A Tisket, A Tasket, My Green and Yellow Basket."

Snyder vs. "Duke" Devaney

As an old trumpet player, I have followed the fortunes of the Cornhusker marching bands since delivering Prof. Don Lentz's newspaper in the 1930s and seeing the band and my cousin, cornet player Lee Stoner from Ravenna, board the train for Pasadena and the Rose Bowl in 1940.

So it was very enjoyable for me to work with Don Lentz's successor Jack Snyder, and other directors, when I had major Stadium responsibilities on game day. A key band staff member still is Rose Johnson, who has been a great help in coordinating events with the athletic department through the years.

Snyder is a wonderful musician, an outstanding director, and has long been a leader in music education. I found out at the Sun Bowl in 1969 that my friend Jack is one tough cookie, too.

He went toe-to-toe one afternoon in El Paso with Coach Bob Devaney, who picked up Depression-era spending money boxing as "Duke" Devaney. No blows were struck, but Jack won the battle.

The Sun Bowl Committee apparently made a booking error, and when the Nebraska football team arrived at the practice site, the field was covered by the Cornhusker marching band. Devaney told Snyder to vamoose, and Jack told Bob to go fly a kite. Despite Bob's protestations, Snyder would not stop the band and depart the field.

So the band played on, and the football team reboarded the buses. Sun Bowl officials found a new practice site for Coach Devaney, who never really liked to lose at anything. Nebraska defeated Georgia, 45-6, and the band put on a great show, thus preserving the friendship between the two combatants.

Gordon MacRae Opens the Door

Nebraska football fans were treated to some outstanding entertainment at Memorial Stadium thanks to Gordon MacRae.

MacRae skyrocketed to singing and movie fame in "Oklahoma," and continued to star in many movies and personal appearances. In addition to being an outstanding entertainer, Gordon was a great guy. We met

Gordon MacRae (Photo courtesy of University of Nebraska)

after he and his wife Liz moved to Lincoln, and he continued performing in all parts of the nation.

Gordon became a real fan of the Nebraska football team, and he expressed interest in singing the National Anthem at a football game. It struck me as a great idea, and Bob Devaney thought so, too. I checked with the band staff, and they were less than enthusiastic, because the band had always played the Anthem, and the fans did the singing. Also, there was a question about the band accompanying a singer without practice due to the microphone feedback.

Simple solution: Gordon MacCrae would sing *a capella*. He certainly did, and it was a sensational, moving rendition. The crowd cheered, and a Husker tradition was born. Whenever Gordon could be in Lincoln for a game, he'd call me, and I would let the band know MacRae was available to sing the Anthem. That went on for several years until Gordon became ill with cancer and could no longer sing. No one ever performed the National Anthem better than Gordon did at Memorial Stadium in his prime. At Gordon's funeral in Lincoln, his daughter, Meredith, recalled one of Gordon's proudest moments, and it occurred at Memorial Stadium.

His last appearance was the most moving. Meredith, a star in her own right, was in Lincoln and asked if she and her father could sing a duet. Quickly booked, they stood together on the field. It was very near the end of his career, and on the sideline I sensed they both realized they might never sing together again.

Tears glistened in their eyes as they sang the Anthem, and afterward, eyes shining with excitement through the tears, Gordon said, "Fox, that meant so much to sing with Meredith, here for all these Nebraskans. That was one of the biggest thrills ever. Thank you for letting us sing together out there."

Gordon MacRae's appearance at Memorial Stadium had unexpected consequences, in addition to enthusiastic appreciation given his singing by the fans.

Both the band and athletic departments began getting requests from choir singers, rock singers, music teachers, and piano bar singers for a chance to sing the National Anthem at Memorial Stadium. No way did either department want to go down that road. We could not audition singers, nor could we take a chance on an unknown vocalist, unfamiliar with the public address time delay, laying an egg at the Stadium. So we established a policy that we would not permit anyone to sing the National Anthem who was not a national movie, stage, or recording star.

That let Gordon MacRae in, but ended the problem of saying no to amateurs wanting to audition at Memorial Stadium. Happily, however, the appearances of MacRae and the new policy led to several other well-known performers taking the spotlight before Cornhusker games.

Joe Feeney, a Nebraska native who starred on the "Lawrence Welk Show" for many years, later sang the National Anthem. One amateur made the lineup, when wingback star Anthony Steels wanted to sing the Anthem before the Oklahoma game in 1980. Coach Tom Osborne gave his approval for Anthony to miss the final pregame session in the locker-room, and Anthony gave an outstanding rendition of the Anthem, much to the delight of the crowd. His singing did inspire the Huskers, but the Sooners won the game, 21-17. Anthony sang again in his senior season.

A Stirring Rendition

Nebraska may have an exclusive on pregame National Anthem presentations. At least, I don't know of other school—at least in Division I-A—that has had the Star-Spangled Banner played by a pianist.

World-famed pianist Van Cliburn honored the University of Nebraska by playing the National Anthem on a Steinway Grand piano at Memorial Stadium just before the kickoff of a Husker game. Cliburn gave a sensational rendition that rolled from the public address system in stirring fashion. How the event came to pass still ranks as a major miracle.

I knew Van Cliburn was in Lincoln for a concert at the Lied Center for Performing Arts, but it never dawned on anyone that the great artist would play the National Anthem at the football game. However, in athletic administration, you learn to be flexible. I was hosting the Friday night press party, when I received a phone call from D.B. "Woody" Varner, former Chan-

Don Bryant meeting Van Cliburn. (Photo courtesy of University of Nebraska)

cellor, later President of the University of Nebraska and then Chair of the University of Nebraska Foundation.

"Don, I think we can get Van Cliburn to play the National Anthem tomorrow, and we are working some arrangements," Woody said. "We need to get a piano and a place to put it on the sidelines, so we'll need some help."

Woody called later to tell me the piano was found, and we were go for the mission.

Early the next morning, I joined maintenance people and music people at the Stadium where a platform was installed. The Steinway arrived and placed on the platform; the piano was wired for the PA system. A big concern was getting the piano off the sideline without delaying the opening kickoff, so I contacted the game officials. They looked the setup over and were assured that the kickoff would not be delayed.

Mister Cliburn arrived, checked everything over, and visited with the workmen. He seemed very at ease and excited about playing to a football crowd for the first time. The band show started, and the crowd was surprised when it was announced Van Cliburn would perform the National Anthem. He received thunderous ovations before and after his performance.

After the last note, work crews quickly moved the piano and the platform while the NU Band completed its show, and the two teams ran on the field. The kickoff was held on schedule and a history-making Nebraska football event had been achieved on short notice.

The Marching Aggies

Marching bands have always played a big part in the overall excitement of college football games.

One of the big pluses when the Big Eight Conference joined with four Texas teams to form the Big 12 Conference, was the addition of Texas A&M. The Aggie marching band is one of most impressive musical units in college football, certainly one of my favorite bands. Watching the Texas A&M band perform almost makes me want to reenlist in the Marines.

The Cornhusker marching band is a tremendous group of more than 350 musicians, and it adds a great deal to Husker football seasons. One of my biggest thrills ever was to be invited to direct the NU Band in its December concert at Kimball Hall. Of course, the members did not know I was an old professional trumpet player (dance bands) and former member of the American Legion Drum and Bugle Corps. They took a chance anyway, and I conducted the band in "Hail Varsity," long an NU spirit song.

I was asked to say a few words to the audience after completing my tour with the baton. I explained my directing expertise came from an airplane trip from London to New York en route from the Sarajevo Winter Olympic Games in 1984. "I learned a great deal sitting beside John Phillip Sousa III, the grandson of the immortal March King on an airplane!"

8

Husker Potpourri

It Ain't Over Till It's Over

Vicki Cartwright is a real veteran of Sports Information wars, having served the University of Nebraska as a secretary and SI office manager for 22 years.

But nothing prepared Vicki for what happened on the Monday morning after the 2000 Nebraska-Colorado game in Lincoln. On the Friday after Thanksgiving, Colorado appeared to have clinched victory on a touchdown pass from Craig Ochs to John Minardi. A two-point conversion made the score 32-31.

With a mere 47 seconds on the clock, Nebraska's Eric Crouch hit four of five passes, two each to Bobby Newcombe and John Gibson, to set up a successful 29-yard field goal by Josh Brown on the final tick of the clock. A miracle 47-yard drive gave Nebraska a 34-31 victory. So, what does all this have to do with Vicki Cartwright?

On Monday morning, Vicki checked the SI office voicemail and was stunned to hear a fan use "every cuss word known" in calling Coach Frank an "idiot", Husker players "a bunch of bums", and Athletic Director Bill Byrne "stupid for hiring Solich."

Vicki was so shocked, she erased the message and continued to check the calls. "A couple of calls later, I heard the same voice," she laughed. "Only this time he was a lot nicer. He said, 'I'm the guy that called to say Frank was an idiot and the players are bums, but I want you to know that I am the idiot! Please apologize to Coach Solich, Bill Byrne, and the players for my call."

Mrs. Cartwright no doubt understood the scenario, saying, "I'll bet the guy called after Colorado scored and looked like a sure winner. Then, after we won the game on the last play, he probably felt sheepish and called back to apologize."

Buyer Beware

Jim Pillen and George Andrews were two outstanding defensive players on the 1978 Nebraska team that upset No. 1 Oklahoma, 17-14, in Lincoln.

Both made All-Big Eight, Pillen at monster back and Andrews at defensive end. Andrews also was named All-America and both made Academic All-America. Pillen was a hero of the win over Oklahoma, recovering Billy Sims' fumble after Jeff Hansen jarred the ball lose in the final minutes of the game.

Sun Bowl president Allen Rash with Husker Academic All-Americans Jim Pillen and George Andrews (Photo courtesy of the Sun Bowl)

Andrews and Pillen were invited to the 1978 Sun Bowl game in El Paso, Texas, where Academic All-America plaques were given out at half-time. The Huskers headed to Miami for the rematch with Oklahoma, and I escorted the two Academic stars to El Paso, promising Coach Tom Osborne I would rush them to Miami as soon as possible.

The night before the Sun Bowl, Andrews and Pillen made a quick trip to Juarez to check out life in Mexico. They returned about 10 p.m., and located me in the hotel coffee shop. Both were excited to show me the great bargains they had bought on their trip across the Rio Grande. Both proudly flashed beautiful rings they had purchased from "some guy on the bridge," and said, "We got these for only $25."

The next morning they both found me again in the coffee shop, and both looked stunned when they said, "Fox, our fingers have turned green." I assured them they would live, and added, "I knew last night your fingers would turn green. I bought a ring like yours from that guy on the bridge many years ago."

All three of us made it to Miami, green fingers and all, and the Academic All-America committee did not request a return of the two Huskers' plaques. As I recall, Pillen remarked on the flight to Miami, "George, think what that guy could have sold us if we weren't Academic All-Americans!"

Cornhuskers Thelma and Louise

One of the strangest—and funniest —requests I ever received came from Lincoln business leader George Abel, a member of 1940 Rose Bowl team and an All-Big Six guard in 1941.

George and his wife Betty were wintering in Rancho Mirage, California, and playing golf at the Sunrise Country Club. Abel's condo overlooked a lake, and the Abels had provided a pair of swans to patrol the lake. The swans were christened Thelma and Louise.

Bad news. An errant golf ball had conked one of the swans, and either Thelma or Louise was dead. George quickly ordered a new swan and called me. He wanted to locate some small Nebraska football helmets. I asked how small, and he said, "Damn small!" He explained that he thought it would be great to outfit the swans with Cornhusker helmets. Not only would they be better protected, it will be good advertising for Nebraska.

It took a while, but I found swan helmets for Thelma or Louise and one or the other's replacement.

Clark's Longest Return

Only two Nebraska football players are officially credited with 105-yard kickoff returns for touchdowns. Ironically, both marks came against Kansas State in October, but 38 years apart.

Owen Frank, a 1999 inductee into the Nebraska Football Hall of Fame, set the mark on October 14, 1911. On October 8, 1949, sophomore Ron Clark matched the record against the K-State Wildcats.

Clark still ranks No. 6 on the career kickoff return chart with 797 yards racked up during 1949-1950 and—after a two-year stint in the service—1954.

But that 105-yard gallop against Kansas State in 1949 wasn't his longest kickoff return.

Clark's longest return came after his Cornhusker career, when he was playing with the alumni team against the varsity in the Spring Game. Ron took the opening kickoff, ran it 87 yards to the end zone, and without breaking stride, sprinted through the end zone into Schulte Field House at the end of the field.

The Ravenna speedster had a simple explanation for the hasty exit: "I had to throw up!"

The "Double QB"

Nebraska may be the only team ever to use two quarterbacks at the same time. It happened in the first game of the 1959 season when the Cornhuskers were matched against the Texas Longhorns in Lincoln.

Aware that Texas had knocked off Bud Wilkinson's Sooners in 1958, Coach Bill Jennings and his staff devised a new innovation to surprise Darrell Royal's Longhorns. It was the highly classified "double quarterback" formation, and it surprised everyone—Texas, the fans, and the officials.

After the Cornhuskers broke the huddle, quarterback Tom Kramer and halfback Pat Fischer both crouched under the center. When the ball was snapped, there really was big-time option football.

"One could hand off to the remaining halfback," Tolly recalls. "Or one could keep it and go one way, with the other going the other way."

Tolly was the senior quarterback, while Kramer had transferred in after playing at California and was expected to fortify the quarterback depth.

*Don Bryant
with former
Husker Pat
Fischer.*

However, Kramer tore his Achilles tendon, and sophomore Ron Meade became Tolly's back-up as well as a place-kicker.

"We never used the "Double QB" after that Texas game," Tolly said.

Referee Cliff Ogden ruled the formation illegal, and Kramer and Tolly and Meade ran conventional plays the rest of the season.

Nebraska's trick formation didn't bother Texas for too long. The Longhorns won, 20-0. Nebraska, helped by the running and kick-returning of speedy halfback Pat Fischer, went on to beat Minnesota, 32-13; Oregon State, 7-6; stage a huge upset of Oklahoma, 25-21; and edge Colorado,   14-12, in a 4-6 season.

Pat Fischer would help beat Oklahoma again in 1960 before heading to a long NFL career with the St. Louis Cardinals and the Washington Redskins. He still holds the NFL record for most starts at cornerback.

9

Memories from the Press Box

"I'VE GOT THE STATS!"

Harry Caray was one of the best known and most popular sportscasters America has ever known. Harry's rendition of "Take Me Out to the Ballgame" during Chicago Cubs games at Wrigley Field may be his most lasting legacy.

However, his legacy at University of Nebraska football games involves a Boy Scout in my son's troop. Harry worked many University of Missouri football games, in addition to covering major league baseball action for the St. Louis Cardinals, and later the Cubs.

In the early years of my SID career, Nebraska had a tiny, ancient press box, with only four radio booths that could only be reached by climbing an iron ladder to the second level. Harry's St. Louis radio station was assigned a booth for a Tiger-Husker game, and the arrival of a famous announcer such as Harry Caray was special. I instructed Tim Wentz from Troop 63, BSA, to be courier and make sure Harry got copies of the statistics in his precarious perch atop the press box.

Midway in the second quarter, Tim came to me and said, "Fox, I think I really screwed up." Asked why, Tim reported, "I climbed the ladder, opened the door to the booth and yelled, 'I've got the stats!' Mr. Caray turned around and said, 'Congratulations, young man! You have just told middle America that YOU HAVE THE STATS!'"

Tim became an Eagle Scout and now is an assistant professor of construction management in the University of Nebraska College of Business Administration.

Caray and the "Bumaroosky Play"

Husker I-back John O'Leary shocked the Missouri Tigers at Columbia in 1975, but he shocked Harry Caray even more.

Prior to the game, Harry asked me to go on the air with him at halftime to chat about the 7-0 Nebraska team. However, he changed his mind.

Late in the second quarter, Coach Tom Osborne called what came to known as the "Bumaroosky Play." It worked to perfection when the ball was snapped to Tony Davis, who handed the ball forward between O'Leary's legs and sprinted right as O'Leary tore around left end for a touchdown.

It was the play that changed the complexion of the game and led to a 30-7 Nebraska victory. When I approached Harry's radio booth at halftime, his producer stopped me and said, "I'm sorry, Fox, Harry says he doesn't need you today. He's so upset about that freak play, we've turned the show back to the station for music during the half."

Great Seat If You Can Get It

Sports information directors didn't have large staffs of assistants in 1963, so I drafted my 10-year-old son Bill for duty on football game day. My office was in the basketball Coliseum, three blocks from the west side of Memorial Stadium, where the press box was perched in the balcony. With no elevators, it was a long walk and a tough climb.

So, with Bill's help, we started early in the morning lugging typewriters, duplicating machines, statistics, speed cards, reams of paper, and other supplies to the press box. Prior to the Colorado game—my first years as SID—we completed stocking the press box before the Stadium opened to the public. I ordered Bill to go sit in the Knot Hole section until it opened to the other youngsters, gave him a press pass in case an usher tried to eject him, and returned topside.

After the game—won by the Huskers, 41-6—my wife asked me why Bill had been on the sideline with the Nebraska team instead of in the Knot Hole bleachers. I told her she was mistaken, and I had placed Bill in the bleachers. Her response: "I know my own son, and he was with the team on the sidelines."

I confronted Bill about the matter, and he confessed that he had sneaked down to the sideline, but he didn't tell the whole story. His hero on the team was a reserve running back, Maynard Smidt, who had befriended him on photo day, and Bill had hoped to see him.

On Monday, during a meeting with Coach Bob Devaney and his staff, I learned the awful truth. In the second quarter, with Nebraska leading by only a touchdown, Bill had gone up to Bob, pulled his coat and asked, "Coach, how is Maynard Smidt playing today?"

Bob laughed and told me, "Bill left quickly when Mike Corgan (backfield coach) looked down and yelled, "Get the hell out of here, you little S.O.B!" Bill always went the other way when he saw Coach Corgan after that.

Today Bill is a weekly newspaper publisher in Nebraska and a member of the Football Writers Association of America. He is the veteran PA announcer in the Sky Box media facility, a long way from the Husker sideline area.

Broeg's Easy Chair on Press Row

Bob Broeg, the retired sports editor of the *St. Louis Post-Dispatch*, is one of the outstanding members of the press corps and a long-time friend. He saw action with the U.S. Marines in World War II, then returned to cover major league baseball, and college and professional football.

His books and press coverage of the St. Louis Cardinals and the University of Missouri football teams of Don Faurot, Dan Devine, and later coaches, brought joy to football fans and fellow media friends.

Nebraska sports information director John Bentley and I teamed to make life more comfortable for Bob on a couple of his visits to cover Missouri-Nebraska football games. Following the war, Broeg had some back problems, and the old Nebraska press box was anything but comfortable. Writers had to sit on long benches, and if anyone had to get up, everyone else had to stop typing and arise. In 1962, Sweet Old Bentley, as John was known, came to Broeg's rescue by reserving an easy chair for him on press row.

A few years later, Missouri SID Bill Callahan advanced the game in Lincoln and mentioned Broeg was having problems with an ulcer. When he arrived in the press box on game day, I presented Bob with a quart of milk for old time's sake.

Title IX and Press Box Changes

With the advent of Title IX, a lot of sports information directors, athletic directors, and male coaches were not prepared for the impending inevitable changes.

I had no particular opposition to women's athletics, but time would prove me wrong about the future enthusiasm for women in   athletics. I also learned I could be insensitive to some issues, like those involving the football press box.

Prior to Title IX, press box media passes carried the message, "No Women or Children Allowed," and the rule was enforced. The press box was an adult male domain—although the printed rule was there to prevent the media from using press box passes for wives and children. When the University of Nebraska built a new and spacious press box in 1967, I never thought of any needs women might have, because women were not allowed in and female writers were few. To this day, my wife does not like to sit in the Don Bryant Media Facility, because she was never welcome in a press box before.

But things began to change. News organizations wanted women to have access to the press boxes. Athletic directors wanted booths in press boxes to entertain their families and boosters. Press boxes became part of VIP facilities and skybox structures.

The *Lincoln Journal* had one of the first women sportswriters before World War II. June Bierbower was a talented writer, but she wasn't allowed to cover the Huskers from the press box. She took notes in the Stadium seats and wrote her stories at home. We worked together after the war before June moved to Pullman, Washington, to join the Washington State University office of public relations.

I made a gross error in judgment during the halftime of a Husker football game. Joining a group of male writers, Shelley Smith of the *Daily Nebraskan*, the

University's student newspaper, complained about the lack of a women's restroom in the press box. I pointed out there was one available one floor above in the VIP section, but she felt strongly one should be on the press level, because there was one for the men.

Everyone laughed, including Shelley, when I flippantly joked, "Well, Shelley, if you're going to write with the guys, you'll have to go with the guys." Oops! Shelley, who has gone on to a fine career as a writer for *Sports Illustrated* and as a national television personality, blasted me for that crack in her column the following week.

It didn't take long for me to arrange to have the photo darkroom replaced by a women's restroom, much to the pleasure of Mrs. Bob Devaney, as well as Shelley and the many other female writers who cover football.

And I no longer joke about serious concerns of women, not even those of my wife of 50 years. This is one old dog who can take coaching.

Women in the Locker Room?

Solving press-box problems that arose with the advent of women joining the sports media field were minimal compared to the bitter battles that arose when women wanted to enter the men's locker rooms.

The University of Nebraska, the coaches, and I were strongly opposed to admitting women into the locker rooms after football games.

Newspapers and wire services deliberately pushed the issue with phone calls and letters threatening court action.

It made no sense to put 150 players in bathrobes to sit around after games in case a female media person walked in a locker room. So, the University of Nebraska banned both sexes from locker rooms and went to interview areas outside the locker rooms. End of problem.

Husker Lady Trailblazers

Christine Anderson is Nebraska's current sports information director, and she is one of the nation's top

Don Bryant and his 30-year-old sportscoat.

SIDs, and the only woman to fill that position at a major college football power. Chris didn't need a Title IX boost to succeed Old Fat Fox, either. She earned it.

A native of Panama, Nebraska, Chris was a student SID at Nebraska four years before graduating and joining the staff full-time. She became assistant SID at Kansas State, then returned to Nebraska for eight years in that position before heading the department in 1997.

Chris has done an outstanding job of developing a top-ranked sports information operation, which has won many honors, while also being a wife and mother of two young sons. Trailblazer June Bierbower would be mighty proud of Husker SID Chris Anderson.

The Okie and the Elevator

On occasion, an SID must rely strictly on physical fitness and stamina, without counting on assistance, when faced with a rugged opponent. Or a rugged opponent's fan.

During a Nebraska-Oklahoma game in the 1970s, the Nebraska press box was somehow invaded by a Sooner fan, who appeared to be (1) an Oklahoma student and (2) drunk with happiness over OU's lead, as well as a huge amount of spirits. I approached the young man and politely asked him to leave the press box and pointed to the elevator.

He responded by telling me where to go, and a serious discussion commenced. When the elevator door opened, I stopped talking and pushed the fan inside, at which point he grabbed my sweater, pulled it over my head, and started beating me with his fists.

I couldn't see, but I was swinging back while standing on one leg and keeping one leg in the air to prevent the elevator door from closing. I yelled for assistance, and the door kept banging on my leg, then opening again.

Help never came. The press box guards gathered to watch the hilarious scene of Fat Fox being hammered in the elevator while the door kept opening and closing.

I finally broke free and escaped from the elevator, and the Sooner fan was last seen as the tired door finally closed.

Pulling Rank in the Press Box

My funniest press box entanglement came following the 1967 Colorado game in Lincoln. The Buffs had lost five straight to the Huskers, but the No. 4 Buffs surprised Bob Devaney's team, 21-16.

About 45 minutes after the game, three celebrating Colorado fans sneaked in a back door to the press box. Each carried a bottle of beer, and the trio was loudly singing, "Glory, Glory, Colorado," the CU fight song.

Busy sportswriters were looking around to see what the noise was all about, and I approached the three men and congratulated them on a fine victory. Also, they were nicely asked to leave.

Their response was an unprintable negative. But I calmly persisted. Then one of the men said, "Do you realize who you're talking to? I'm Colonel Jones of the U.S. Army, this is Captain Smith of the U.S. Navy, and this is Colonel Johnson of the United States Air Force!" (Not their real names.)

I replied, "Hey, it's really nice to meet you guys, I'm Sergeant Bryant of the U.S. Marine Corps—now get your asses on that elevator!"

As they reluctantly entered the elevator, one of the men growled as the door closed, "We should have known you were an enlisted man!"

Keith Jackson's Bathroom

ABC's Keith Jackson and I have been good friends for many years, and not a day goes by that some football fans says, "You knew Keith Jackson, didn't you? We really miss him—he's the best college football announcer ever."

I agree and suggest they move to the PAC-10 area, if they want to hear Keith on a regular basis these days. Since his full-duty retirement in 1999, he confines his football chores to the Far West.

His last Nebraska game was supposed to be at Manhattan, in 1998 when the Huskers played the Kansas State Wildcats. Bill Snyder's K-State No. 2-ranked team popped the Huskers, 40-30, but the most memorable for me was Friday night before the game.

I had the pleasure, on behalf of the University of Nebraska N Club, to present Keith Jackson with an honorary membership in the N Club and a letter jacket.

But that wasn't his last Nebraska game after all. Nebraska dedicated its new skybox complex at the Husker-California game on September 11, 1999. Happily, for me, ABC sent Keith to Lincoln to do the game with another good friend, Bob Griese, and Keith was on hand to join athletic director Bill Byrne in the cer-

Don Bryant and Keith Jackson (Photo courtesy of University of Nebraska)

emony to name the new press box the Don Bryant Media Facility.

Much as I appreciated the honor, the most fun I had was a surprise for Keith. Keith and his wife Turi arrived on Thursday before the game, and he discovered the new TV announcer booth included a private bathroom. At a dinner party, he raved about that luxury, which never before had been provided anywhere, and he also praised the bathroom on Friday. I contacted Nebraska's director of facilities, John Ingram, and asked him to rig up a sign for Keith's bathroom on game day.

Bright and early on Saturday, Keith arrived at the ABC booth and discovered a red sign with white letters:

KEITH JACKSON TOILET FACILITY
Sept. 11, 1999
—Fox.

Since that day, when the University of Nebraska conducts public tours of the skybox building, the most-asked question has been, "When can we see Keith Jackson's bathroom?"

10
Fox Tales

"Foxie"

The most-asked question of Old Fox after 39 years with the University of Nebraska Athletic Department has been: "Can the Huskers win 'em all next fall and be No. 1?"

The next most-asked question is: "How did you get the nickname 'Fox?' "

Hard as it is for most people to believe after seeing me punching new holes in my belt through the years, I was a distance runner at Lincoln High School. Perhaps even more surprising, based on my won-loss record, I once anchored our two-mile relay team to victory at the Thomas Jefferson Relays in Council Bluffs, Iowa. Thanks to some great running by teammates Tom Harley, Jim Mickelson, and Ted Gunderson, I managed to stagger across the finish line first and wobbled down the track after breaking the string held by two TJ High School cheerleaders. One of those string girls

Don Bryant and his "foxie" hat.

jogged after me and escorted me back to the officials at the finish line, and for some reason we both thought it would be more fun watching the rest of the meet from the grandstand.

Another teammate, Bruce Bergquist, learned that my new Iowa friend's last name was Fox, and from that afternoon I was forever christened "Foxie." While I never saw the girl before that spring afternoon and haven't seen her in all the years since, I appreciate her contribution to my life and whatever dubious fame it brought.

After returning from service in the U.S. Marine Corps, I launched a sportswriting career under Norris Anderson, sports editor of *The Lincoln Star*. He noted my expanding waistline and correspondingly expanded my nickname to "Fat Fox," which became the most-often-used identification label by my media friends since 1950. So, I owe a lot to Bergquist and Anderson, and certainly Miss Fox.

Treasure Chest West I'm Not

Bruce Bergquist had another notable impact on my life by ending my acting career. I was assigned the role of "Liz the Floozy" in the letterman's club skit in the annual Joy Night show, and had to appear in a red formal, blonde wig, striped red and white stockings, rouge and lipstick. I was directed to walk across the stage in seductive fashion and not to speak. After the first night's show, Bruce, an All-State quarterback and point guard, urged me to spice up the act the next night.

"Give the boys in the balcony something to cheer about," Bruce urged. Which is how the next show became more spicy. I halted my seductive walk in the middle of the stage, turned to the audience and commenced bumping and grinding. I hollered, "Here's one for the boys in the balcony!" and fired a bump worthy of Treasure Chest West before making my exit.

Lizzie was met in the wings by Coach Ralph Beechner and Principal Hal Mardis, both of whom questioned my sanity and ordered a Monday appearance at Boys Dean Otto Hackman's office on a morals charge and possible expulsion. My life as a drag queen ended amidst the howls and cheers of Bruce and my L Club buddies.

My Start in Sportswriting

Norris Anderson played an even bigger part in my life than just adding "Fat" to "Fox."

We were both Marine Corps veterans at the University of Nebraska after World War II and were in the same Spanish class. Even though I had once played on the Port Chicago Marine team in the Egg Bowl at Petaluma, California, my center play on the Nebraska Freshman team did little to impress Coach George "Potsy" Clark, nor did Track Coach Ed Weir, a Nebraska legend, seem glad to see me after football season.

Having ballooned from 150 to 185 pounds since he last saw me run, he released me from my promise to return from the service and run for the Nebraska track team.

One day after class, Anderson switched from Spanish to English and said, "Face it, Fox—you are too small and not worth a damn as a football lineman, and you are too damn fat to run track! Why don't you come to work for me at *The Lincoln Star?*"

Norrie had succeeded Charles "Cy" Sherman— who christened the Nebraska football team the Cornhuskers in 1900—as sports editor after World War II combat correspondent duty with the Marines in China. His assessment of my athletic future was accurate, and I launched a sportswriting career in January 1949.

"He Didn't Leave the Field Crying"

Ironically, my first by-line in *The Lincoln Star* was on an interview with Ed Weir.

Indoor track season was starting, and Weir was the Huskers' veteran coach after his two-time All America career as a tackle in the 1920s. Ed was renowned as the "first of the red-dogging lineman" on Nebraska teams that beat Knute Rockne's teams in 1923 and 1925.

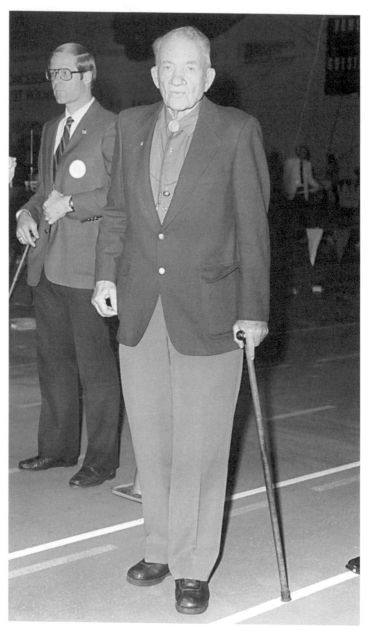

Ed Weir, Nebraska's first two-time All-American.

He was also a standout in the 1924 game with the Irish when the Four Horsemen whipped the Huskers, 34-7. Nebraskans have always bragged about beating the Four Horsemen twice (the only losses Notre Dame suffered during their careers), but frequently forget to mention the game in 1924, when Grantland Rice insured their immortality.

A great high school athlete at Superior, Nebraska, Weir also played a key role in the 1925 victory over Illinois and the Illini's great Harold "Red" Grange. Nebraska legend has always had Grange being held to minus-yards rushing and retreating from the field in tears near the end of the game.

No way! Not according to Weir, a defensive terror who helped ensure a 14-0 win at Champaign that day. He never agreed with the aspersions cast against No. 77 by overzealous fans and inaccurate reporters.

"We didn't hold Red to minus-yards," Ed always maintained. "He was held down to 30 or 40 yards, but that story about minus-yards and leaving the game in tears was not true. We held him down pretty good, but not like the fans and press liked to remember, and he didn't leave the field crying."

Corgan's Helmet

Bob Devaney liked to have some fun toward the end of a game week, and prior to a Colorado game, he decided to pull a joke on backfield coach Mike Corgan. With my assistance and at the risk of incurring Mike's wrath, of course.

I took an ancient (1909) football helmet from a trophy case, put it in a sack, and dropped by the Thursday practice. Bob called the squad together and said that I had an important announcement to make. At

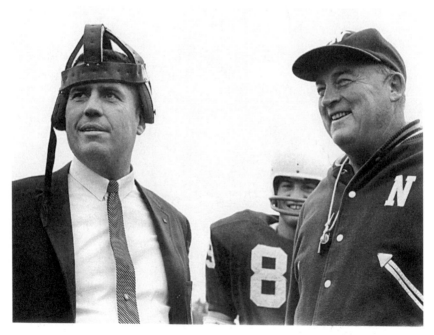

Don Bryant (left) with Bob Devaney. (Photo courtesy of University of Nebraska)

that point, I told the squad that Notre Dame had recently cleared out the old equipment room and sent us Coach Corgan's helmet he used when he played for the Fighting Irish.

Then I pulled out the helmet and put it on my head, causing the players to yell and cheer. Over the cheers, the Nebraska campus heard Coach Corgan yelling, "Why you little fat son of a bitch!" Much to Devaney's delight, the squad whooped it up even more. And Mike Corgan and I became very good friends.

Bring Me a Note

One of the big responsibilities sports information directors had after World War II was "advancing" their schools' athletic contests, particularly football games.

An SID would load a briefcase with press releases, media brochures, film clips of movie action, statistics, and photos of star players, and hit the road for out-of-town games. Some would leave early in the week, depending upon the importance of the games, while a trip might be delayed until a day or two before a game of lesser importance.

In theory, advancing was done to 1) use the media contacts to generate interest in your team and the game, which might transmit into ticket sales; and 2) maintain good relations with the media which would help accomplish publicity that would help boost ticket sales—always a high priority of athletic directors.

In fact, advancing was 1) tiring (lugging a heavy briefcase and a heavy portable typewriter; 2) irritating to SID wives; 3) good for generating friendships with media people and staff people at other schools; and 4) enticing some fans to the game, which made ADs happy.

When Bob Devaney became athletic director at Nebraska, he laid down only one rule about advancing football games: "I don't care when you leave town, but if you leave before Sunday, you've got to bring me a note from your wife!"

A Ticket for a Prayer

Visiting media outlets wasn't my only responsibility when I advanced road games.

Nebraska teams under Bob Devaney and Tom Osborne always provided game-day church opportunities for the players and staff members who wished to participate.

John Melton, an assistant with Devaney at Wyoming and Nebraska, who also served many years with Osborne, was the church coordinator for the Catholic services. I could always expect a phone call on the road from John, "Foxie, don't forget, we need a priest for Saturday!"

I checked many phone books in strange cities through the years, and I always managed to find a priest for John. Tom Osborne was closely involved with the

Fellowship of Christian Athletes and usually coordinated the Protestant services.

One thing helped me a great deal during my search for priests willing to hold pre-game Mass for the "enemy team." I offered breakfast with the team during the pre-game meal and a ticket to the game.

"Pepping Up" the Wrong Side

Sometimes "advancing" a football game created interesting—if not unexpected—incidents that led to inspiring an opposing team.

Nebraska played Air Force at Colorado Springs in 1965, and I spent the week in Denver making media rounds, press luncheons and speaking to civic and booster groups. Late in the week, I was invited to become the first non-Air Force person to address the Cadet Corps pep rally.

Friday night, adorned in a red blazer, I joined the Academy student body for dinner and then moved outside the dining hall for the rally. Falcon players spoke to the group and fired everyone up with promises of a heavy bombing attack on the Cornhuskers. Finally, I was introduced, and the Cadet Corps gave me a booing welcome to the Academy.

I countered by saying, "Hey, guys, I served in the Armed Forces of the United States of America—that's the same team you guys are on."

No laughs, but a lot of loud chatter and snickers came forth from the restless cadets.

Figuring it was time to have some fun, I next said, "Hey, guys, I understand when you graduate from the Air Force Academy you will all be commissioned second lieutenants in the United States Air Force!"

Boy, did they clap and cheer on that one. Until I added, "Hey, guys, I held the equivalent rank—I was a staff sergeant in the United States Marine Corps!"

Fortunately, some Air Police kept the crowd back as the Falcon Faithful went into attack formation.

The next day, Husker fullback Frank Solich (who would become Nebraska's head coach in 1998) ran 80 yards for a touchdown on the first play of the game and scored two more times. But Ben Martin's Falcons battled back to press the Huskers in the second half before losing, 27-17.

In the locker room after the game, Coach Bob Devaney asked me, "What the hell did you say out here this week?" When I told him about having a good time kidding the cadets at the pep rally, Bob shook his head and said, "From now on, I'll tell you what to say!"

And I don't think Air Force has had a non-family member address a pep rally since.

After inspiring Air Force to give the Cornhuskers a mighty effort in 1965, I was careful on future advance trips. So in 1966, I checked with Coach Devaney before the Iowa State and Wisconsin trips. When I checked with Bob before my return to Colorado, where the Huskers would meet Eddie Crowder's Buffaloes in Boulder, he indicated a fierce desire to beat the Buffs and said, "Tell them to screw their hats on tight!"

I thought he was kidding, but he said, "We're good, and we'll get after them. It will be a great game—tell them to screw their hats on tight, we'll show up."

Although I was still apprehensive, during an early week media luncheon, Denver writers speculated that CU was loaded and gunning for the Huskers.

So I responded by saying, "I know the Buffs are good, but Nebraska's a pretty good team. They better have their hats screwed on tight." That good-natured response wound up in print—and on the Colorado bulletin board—and once again I was in trouble.

Heading to the fourth quarter, Colorado led Nebraska, 19-7, and Buff players were suggesting to NU players that they should "screw their hats on tight." I headed for the locker room, figuring I'd be fired, and did not see the end of the game. However, in the dying moments of the battle, Husker fullback Pete Tatman capped a last-quarter comeback with a touchdown to give Nebraska a 21-19 victory.

When the team burst into the locker room cheering, I learned about the win and felt I might be able to at least ride home on the team plane.

But my fear of being fired eased when Coach Devaney walked by me and said in a low voice, "From now on, we'll both keep our damned mouths shut."

To this day, whenever I see former Nebraska basketball great Bus Whitehead during football season, he asks me, "Have you told the other team to screw their hats on tight this week?"

The Amazing Flea-Flicker

Barry Switzer and his Sooner players gave me one of greatest shows I've ever seen, and it didn't take place in a football game. It happened in 1977 during a run-through practice on Thanksgiving Day in Norman.

Barry had invited me to have Thanksgiving dinner with his staff and players because I was advancing the Friday game. The Nebraska team was to arrive in Norman and follow the Oklahoma team's brief practice, so I went to Owen Field after dining with the Sooners. It was a loose group of Sooners getting ready before the run-through became serious. Some big linemen smoked cigars, other players were tossing Frisbees. A little Thanksgiving Day fun before the big game with Nebraska the next day, I thought, while sitting on the west sideline bench.

But I hadn't seen anything yet. Barry blew his whistle and yelled, "Fox, come out here," waving me to the middle of the field. He called his top offensive unit over and informed them, "This is the Fat Fox from Nebraska. He's a good guy, one of us. Now run the flea-flicker play for Fox!"

Now, I was hurting. In 1976 OU had stunned the Huskers, 20-17, in Lincoln with a last-minute flea-flicker play, and now I didn't know what to expect.

But it was worth the pain. The Sooner offense broke a huddle and snapped the ball. The quarterback flipped the ball out to a receiver who lateraled the ball to a back running by and someone shouted, "Stop! Reverse!"

The guy with the ball ran backwards, got the back to the receiver, who backed up and got the ball to the quarterback, who got the ball back to the center, and the whole unit backed up to the huddle. It was like watching a movie projector, forward and backward, and that wasn't the first time the Sooners had performed that number.

And the next day, Barry and the OU Sooners beat Nebraska, 38-7. However, they didn't need the flea-flicker.

Bill McCartney Sees Red

Sometimes the hospitality encountered by sports information   directors advancing road games was less than in places like Oklahoma, LSU, and Auburn.

It was downright chilly—or even cold—in Colorado during Bill McCartney's reign as the head coach of the University Colorado Buffaloes.

Bill announced as soon as he checked out his Buff whistle that Nebraska was Colorado's "No. 1 Rival."

Husker games were printed in red on Colorado sched-
ules, and CU fans were invited to despise their hated
neighbors to the East. Colorado media people went
on the warpath against the Huskers and had a ball in-
sulting Coach Tom Osborne and the Nebraska players
and fans.

Some of the Nebraska-bashing media material was
distasteful and even vulgar, while others came up with
some really humorous attacks on Nebraska.

Husker coach Tom Osborne drove the Buffs and
their media daffy by downplaying the "rivalry". It infu-
riated the CU team, their fans, and media when
Osborne would say, "We respect Colorado, but we look
at Colorado the same as any other game. Every game
we play is a big game, so we don't want to view Colorado any differently than we do other opponents."

My favorite Colorado media jab at Nebraska came
while I was driving through Denver to the Tuesday Big
Three Media luncheon before a Nebraska-Colorado
game. A radio talk show was going strong and stressing
the excitement and huge build-up of the game. The
host said, "We are really lucky to have both Coach Bill
McCartney of Colorado and Tom Osborne of Nebraska
with us today, so we can get the inside on how these
two great teams are getting ready for Saturday's gigan-
tic battle in Boulder. . . . First up is Coach McCartney."

The station played a tape of a McCartney interview in which Bill talked about how big the game was
and how excited his players and staff were about playing Nebraska.

"Thanks, Bill, and good luck to the Buffs on Saturday," the host said. "And now, let's hear from Nebraska coach Tom Osborne. Good morning, Tom, how do you view this week's big game with Colorado?"

What followed was a tape of a man snoring very loudly, and I almost wrecked the car laughing so hard.

Bill McCartney really got into the anti-Nebraska syndrome and, with the help of that enthusiasm and some outstanding players, he beat the Huskers three times. Bill's Buffs had a great 1990 season, beating Nebraska, 27-12, and winning a national championship.

Larry Zimmer of station KOA in Denver is an old friend and one of the most respected play-by-play announcers in the business. Larry and his wife Bridget are always on my radio booth must-stop list when Colorado and Nebraska play.

I learned how serious Coach McCartney was about hating the color red when I was asked to be a guest on his weekly coach's show from a bar in Boulder. There was a heavy snow storm blowing through Boulder, and I wore an Olympic sweater from Sarajevo for warmth. Never thinking about flashing red at the coach, I arrived at the bar wearing a red wool sweater, with one big white stripe and one big blue stripe.

When Bill arrived, he looked at me and said, "You know better than to wear red around here!"

I responded with a smile and said, "Hi, coach, it's red, white and blue—America, the side we're both on."

Bill McCartney did a great deal for CU's program, and no one was more surprised than Old Fox with his unexpected resignation.

Kush and Son

Former Arizona State football coach Frank Kush has long been one of the good guys in coaching, and it was a kick for me when he was voted into the College Football Hall of Fame.

Kush and his son, Dan, teamed to beat Nebraska in the 1975 Fiesta Bowl, 17-14. Dan kicked two field goals and a pair of PATs, and his second field goal with 4:50 left in the game knocked off the No. 6 Huskers.

Frank broke up the audience in South Bend, Indiana, during his enshrinement at the College Football Hall of Fame. Noting that people often wondered why he had his son, Dan, as the starting kicker for the Sun Devils, Kush said, "He really wasn't a great kicker, but my wife told me, 'If Dan doesn't play, you don't play!' "

"Ho, Ho, Ho"

Sometimes a sports information director must perform duties above and beyond the call of duty or job description. One year in Miami, Fat Fox was pressed into service as Santa Claus, and it was a tough trip from the North Pole.

Bob Devaney's team was headquartered at the Ivanhoe Hotel in the Bal Harbor area of Miami Beach, and the manager wanted to hold a Christmas party for the children of the Husker staff and those of the hotel staff. Since I would require less padding than anyone else, assistant coach Jim Ross nominated me, Devaney seconded, and I was elected.

On the afternoon of the party, the Ivanhoe manager delivered a costume to my room, and I was transformed into Santa Claus. Game Plan: I was to use the freight elevator to descend to the mezzanine level and await the signal to appear at the top of the grand staircase. I had a heavy bag of toys to lug, and after yelling, "Ho-ho-ho," I was to move down the stairs to meet the children and distribute gifts.

The mezzanine level served as the team dining room, but when I arrived to await my entrance, it had become a ballroom, and a crowd of people were gathered to celebrate someone's 50th wedding anniversary. The happy groom spotted Santa Claus and rushed over and asked me to meet the bride, which I did, and the crowd urged Santa to dance with the bride.

The orchestra struck up "Anniversary Waltz," and we twirled around the room. It was tough for me, because I had once flunked the Arthur Murray two-step course. When we finished, the groom noticed Santa was sweating and insisted he drink a Scotch and water. Still no call came for my entrance, and other women lined up to dance with Santa. Of course, more Scotch was consumed, and soon my beard was soaking wet.

Finally, my cue came, and I staggered down the steps with my load of gifts and Scotch as the "Anniversary" guests cheered and the children wondered how Santa Claus got so wet. I mentioned heavy snow at the North Pole, but only the Nebraska kids understood snow.

When my son Bill came through the gift line, I gave a weak "Ho-Ho," and he said softly, "You're looking good, Fox!" Of course, my wife had a different impression, but we still had a Merry Christmas in Miami.

On the Recruiting Trail

NCAA rules now prohibit coaches and athletic staff members from personally signing recruits on Commitment Day. But it wasn't like that in the 1960s and 1970s. Coaches would travel all over the country on Signing Day to make sure recruits and their parents inked letters of intent.

Recruiting became part of my job description on Signing Day, both for Bob Devaney and Tom Osborne, before the rules changed. Offensive line coach Cletus Fischer coordinated recruiting in Nebraska and would assign me to drive around the state to bring back signed letters from high school players he had recruited. In most cases, I never had met the recruits, nor did I know what Cletus had discussed with the families during recruiting.

In 1965 I went to Beatrice and signed Joe Armstrong, who became an All-America guard in 1968. In 1968 I drove to Columbus to sign Bill Kosch, who would be an all-conference defensive back on the 1970 and 1971 national championship Husker teams. His parents didn't sign the letter of intent until two questions they had were cleared up.

Mrs. Kosch wanted to make sure Bill would have facilities to do his laundry, while Mr. Kosch asked about the availability of church opportunities on campus. I assured them on both counts, and we all enjoyed coffee in the kitchen. Bill Kosch's son Jesse ranks as the No. 2 career punter at Nebraska. Jesse lettered in 1994-95-96-97, and his punting contributed to the Huskers' three national titles.

The Porter family in Nebraska City boasts a long history of Nebraska football tradition, as well as a famous relative—J. Sterling Morton, the Secretary of Interior who established Arbor Day. His mansion in Nebraska City, Arbor Lodge, is a national historic treasure. It sits across the highway from the apple orchards the Porter family operated for many years.

G.M. Porter lettered in football in 1914, and his son, Morton, lettered in 1943. Morton's son, Scott, was a fullback letterman for Tom Osborne in 1983-84. Scott's older brother, Budge, was a promising Husker recruit before a catastrophic neck injury ended his career. I never met Scott before he reported for football practice, but I brought back his letter.

After the NCAA rules changed, it would have been a violation if I met him on Signing Day. So I stayed in the high school athletic director's office while Scott and his parents signed the letter of intent. The AD brought the document to me, and I drove back to Lincoln.

Coach Devaney had me go with him to Omaha to help sign up recruit Adrian Fiala, who became a standout linebacker in 1967-68-69 and later a lawyer. He is an analyst on the Pinnacle Sports Husker football and baseball radio networks these days.

Among other signers I bagged were Chuck Jones (1974-75 defensive back) from Beatrice; Greg Jorgensen (1975-76-77), a senior co-captain from Minden; and Tony Davis (1973-74-75), a bruising running back from Tecumseh.

Bob Logsdon, the manager of the Lincoln Legionnaire Club and a native of Tecumseh, was so happy Davis was going to be a Husker, he accompanied me to the signing at the high school. After Tony signed, Bob ordered me to head for the Rock Acres Saloon, where he called friends, including the mayor, the police chief, and others, to join us for a celebration.

Tough Tony never let us down. He sparked the Huskers to a 40-13 win over UCLA in his and Tom Osborne's first game, and had a fine career. His son, Josh, a Colorado sprint champion, followed dad to NU in 1999.

Hail to the Chief

The euphoria surrounding Nebraska's first national football championship didn't end when the Cornhuskers flew home from Miami after beating Louisiana State, 17-12, in the Orange Bowl.

It peaked a few weeks later when President Richard Nixon came to Lincoln to present a plaque to Coach Bob Devaney, co-captains Dan Schneiss and Jerry Murtaugh, and the University of Nebraska.

I was attending the NCAA convention when a phone call from my secretary informed me that the president was coming to Nebraska.

I flew home, walked into my office, and discovered it had been stripped: furniture, pictures, and files had been removed to prepare my Coliseum office to be the president's "Ready Room" Spotting a table with three phones on it, I lifted one receiver and heard a voice say, "Please hang up immediately, this is a White House telephone."

It wasn't long before I met some very nice secret service men. During the days leading up to President Nixon's visit, there were some heated exchanges between White House staff members—some who would become associated with Watergate—and the Secret Service men. If I were scoring, I'd say the White House lost most of the time because of security reasons, but the Secret Service took some abuse.

Nebraska was No. 1 again in 1971, beating both No. 2 Oklahoma and No. 2 Alabama. President Nixon honored the Huskers again, this time at the White House. Coach Bob Devaney, co-captains Jim Anderson and Jerry Tagge, and All-America players joined Nebraska Senator Carl Curtis in the Oval Office for a ceremony.

In 1982, I met President Nixon for the last time, and he had not forgotten his visit to Lincoln in January 1971. During the reception prior to the National Football Foundation's annual banquet at the Waldorf Astoria Hotel in New York, I was standing near the door when Mr. Nixon walked in and smiled. I said, "Good evening, Mr. President," and we shook hands.

I explained I was with the University of Nebraska, and he became enthusiastic and said, "Oh, yes, I came out there to honor Bob Devaney and his great team, and you came back to the White House the next year. And, oh, that Rimington boy you have now—he's a great player!"

The Duke

John Wayne has always been one of my favorite movie stars, while my female vote goes to Maureen O'Hara, especially since they both starred in my favorite movie, "The Quiet Man."

So, it was a particular thrill when I met the former Southern California football player at the National Football Foundation and College Football Hall of Fame dinner in New York.

But we didn't have a long conversation. He was talking with a group at the pre-dinner reception when one of group motioned me over and said, "John, this is Don Bryant from Nebraska."

We shook hands and he said, "Hiya, Don," and I said, "It's great to meet you Mr. Wayne," as the lights blinked to announce dinner.

But I'll always remember he sounded just like "Duke" Wayne.

Michener Magic

After years of reading books like *Hawaii*, *Texas*, and *Centennial*, James Michener became my favorite author. But I never expected to get a phone call from him.

However, in early December of 1988, I answered my phone and heard, "Don, this is James Michener, and I need your help." My initial reaction was, "Yeah, sure—what's the gag?" But he continued, "Norris Anderson told me to call you." Since Anderson gave me my first newspaper job, and I knew he was in Miami, I said, "Great to hear from you, Mr. Michener." It turned out to be on the level and a fun experience.

Mr. Michener explained that since Nebraska was coming to Miami for the Orange Bowl, he wanted some help in locating a Nebraska fan. "When I wrote *Sports in America*, I included a story about a great Nebraska fan, and I would like to know if he is coming to the Orange Bowl," he said. "If he is, I want to take him to lunch."

He couldn't recall the man's name, but I promised to help. I checked the book and noted that the author was referring to Russell Swanson of Omaha. I checked the Nebraska ticket office and learned Swanson had ordered Orange Bowl tickets. I called him and verified his trip, then got back to Michener, and the luncheon was arranged.

On media day at the Orange Bowl, Norris Anderson brought Mr. and Mrs. Michener to the Orange Bowl, and I had a long visit with my favorite author. Coach Tom Osborne brought his *Texas* book to practice and had it autographed. My wife met Mr. Michener later, and stills claims that was her biggest bowl trip thrill.